D1519041

Riding the Elephant

An Alzheimer's Journey

Diane Porter Goff

Dreamsplice
Christiansburg, Virginia

This book is not a work of fiction. All of the events are reported as recalled by the author. The names of some non-family members have been changed.

An excerpt from the chapter entitled "Acquainted with the Night" appeared in the anthology, *Beyond Forgetting: Poetry and Prose about Alzheimer's Disease* (Kent State University Press, 2009). Reprinted with permission.

RIDING THE ELEPHANT: An Alzheimer's Journey

Copyright © 2009 by Dreamsplice

Dreamsplice
3462 Dairy Road
Christiansburg, VA 24073

www.dreamsplice.com

Cover design by Larkin Porter Goff
Front Cover photo by Diane Porter Goff
Back Cover photo by Richard M. Goff

ISBN: 978-0-9761559-3-5
Library of Congress Control Number: 2009925899
First Edition

Printed in the United States of America by
Instantpublisher.com

This book is for all those whose lives have been touched by Alzheimer's disease.

And for my sister, Beverly, who rode with me all the way.

In the midst of winter, I finally learned that there was in me an invincible summer.

Albert Camus

Acknowledgments

I applaud my family for being the wellspring of this book. Besides walking with me throughout the journey with Mama, their unswerving interest, devotion and sense of humor supplied the impetus to keep me writing the story down. My husband, Richard, and daughter, Larkin, provided emotional support and always took the time to listen to my first drafts. My sister, Beverly Simpson, always my finest critic, went over the manuscript many times and used her English teacher skills to hone it into a finer configuration. My nieces, Sarah Baines and Rachel Shockley, offered encouragement and cheerleading, not to mention memory checks and details. My brother-in-law, Ed Simpson, Jr. and nephew, Ed Simpson III, proffered bouts of humor, sometimes with my nephew sporting one of Mama's hats.

I'll always treasure the memory of all of us women sitting around my sister's kitchen, recalling stories of the "Alzheimer's years" and laughing and crying together. My family always sanctioned the feeling that "our" story was meant to go beyond the bonds of family and be shared with the world.

Many people participated in the production of this book. The manuscript first took shape under the competent wing of Judy Bridges, founder of Redbird Studio in Milwaukee, with help from the members of several Writers' Roundtables. The book continued to evolve with guidance from Amanda Cockrell and her classes at Hollins University. Thanks also to Catherine Van Noy, who inspired me during our trips down the mountain to our Hollins classes.

Much gratitude goes to my friend and fellow writer, Ann, who furnished superb editing and feedback and kept the flame of writing alight in my daily life. I'm also grateful to the other readers who tendered suggestions—Mary, Elizabeth, Katy and Ethel Marie. And kudos to Bob at Dreamsplice, for his expertise, thoroughness and deadline coaching throughout the final pages.

And most of all, thanks to Daddy and Mama, for their vital spirit that still infuses our lives.

D.P.G.

Bath Time

Her fragile little body sits upright in the water, legs stuck straight out like a child's. Mama has always liked her baths hot and now, with old age sitting in her bones, she likes them even hotter. Steam rises. Rivulets run down the pink tiles surrounding the tub and the small mirror above the sink is fogged over. Her narrow ranch house bathroom shimmers like a wet bubble, delicately infused with the smell of lavender soap. For this bath time, I have stripped down to my bra and a pair of shorts.

We begin with her hair. She holds a blue washcloth over her closed eyes with both hands while I palm on the shampoo and lather up her short haircut into soft peaks like meringue on pie. At ninety, Mama's hair is still replete with brown, the grey shining through in swatches. Fine and thin, it earned the name "frog hair" from Mama's cousin who was a hair stylist.

I can sit on the closed toilet lid and reach both the sink and Mama, easily getting clean water from the sink for rinsing out the suds with a large plastic cup. The stream runs down over Mama's back—the slightly hunched shoulders, the pearl string of the spine—and down over her front, her old mastectomy scar on the left, the sharp ribs showing through where the soft breast should be, the skin folded over and sewn like the thick, crooked hem in a skirt.

I remember how she spoke that night, long after I thought she was asleep, into the dim light of the hospital recovery room. "I wonder where it is," she said in her matter-of-fact tone.

I leaned over and felt in the covers for her hand. "What, Mama?"

She gazed past me toward the ceiling, not returning my hand squeeze.

"My breast. I wonder where it is." She turned her blue-green eyes to mine. "Did they just throw it out in the trash?"

I had no answer.

I wonder now if she remembers that moment or if the ugly barbed broom of Alzheimer's disease has swept it out the doorway of her mind like so many other memories.

"Does it squeak yet?" Her question brings me back to the bathroom.

"One more rinse." Warm water bubbles into the cup and I sluice her head again. "Now, let's see." I take a piece of her wet hair between my forefinger and thumb and pinch down on it until it emits a squeaking sound. "All done. It squeaks!"

She wipes the washcloth down over her face and pops open her eyes. "Good and clean!" she exclaims with a satisfied air. She splashes the rag vigorously up and down in the water, plies it with soap, then bends forward and begins methodically washing each of her toes.

I straighten up and stretch out my cramped back, push my reddish hair back from my wet forehead. My red hair and freckles were an anomaly in my family and my older sister had me convinced I was adopted until I realized my nose was an exact replica of Mama's. Both swoop down in ski jump fashion and widen at the end with a slight crease in the tip. Mama, who always said she was a mix of English, High Irish and Low Irish, called this configuration "the Low Irish nose."

My upper torso is dripping, either from the steamy water or a hot flash that has sneaked up on me. Droplets of moisture spot the mural I painted on the inside of the door when I was fifteen. In the painting a pink flamingo-like bird raises its beak up toward its mother that leans down, both their necks undulating in identical S curves. Their pronged feet grasp onto gray rocks while willow branches frame the top of the scene. Even though the bathroom has been painted several times, Mama has insisted the mural not be changed. Five years ago she asked me to come over and touch up the colors. I couldn't get the pink paint light enough so I repainted the whole scene again, carefully staying within the lines.

I stare at the mural and think of the time I sent two amateur paintings to Mama from college and the next time I came home they were beautifully framed and hanging on the living room walls. I recall how she accepted with equanimity my decision to enter the Peace Corps at age twenty-one. No matter what unusual forays I made into life—a wedding planned in four days, commune living, motorcycle racing, macrobiotics—Mama never blinked. Daddy used to say, with a tinge of irritation in his voice, "If Diane came home riding on an elephant, Mama would build a garage for it."

Maybe this excursion into the land of dementia is the next elephant ride. I get a sudden mental picture of my sister, Mama and me atop a huge pachyderm, "Alzheimer's Express" tattooed in red letters across its tough, hairy side. Whatever it was to be, Beverly and I had agreed, Mama wasn't making the journey alone. We would be there for the duration. We had no idea how arduous, how sad, and at times, how hilarious the trip was going to be.

The sound of splashing turns me around. Mama is struggling to get up. "No, Mama, wait. Let me help you." Her body is slick with soapy water as I help her out of the tub. I dry her off, sprinkle on the floral powder she loves and wrap her in a fluffy blue towel. "Come on, Mama, let's get you dressed and get back on that elephant."

She turns her fresh scrubbed face to mine. The creases in her neck shine white with powder. "Elephant? Is that a word I know?"

Beginnings

Mama was no stranger to illness. She contracted whooping cough on the day she was born, January 2, 1908. Their family doctor said he knew she caught it then because she "whooped" six days later. Six is the exact number of days needed to incubate the disease. The whooping sound erupted from her tiny throat like the cross between a rattle and a swoosh. "Whooping" was a sign dreaded by the people of those times—a sign that this often-fatal disease had taken hold.

Her maternal grandmother, Ada, always said it was her fault, that she had brought the sickness to the newborn on her apron. No one in that large, extended family knew the theory of germs, but Ada had been at home bending over the youngest of her ten children who was already ill with the disease when another daughter burst in the door, bringing news that the first grandchild of the family had been born. Without changing her apron, Ada walked swiftly out the door, down across the snow-blown yard, straight into the little house where her third daughter, Dallas, lifted up the delicate bud of a girl for her to hold.

"I just feel like the sickness was on my apron, somehow." Ada bemoaned in the days that followed, as she and her six healthy daughters took turns night and day, sitting beside small Dorris Evelyn as she panted and struggled her way through the illness.

Dorris' father, Jimmy, also sat beside her in the wee hours. Her mother told her later how he would reach his slim finger into her tiny throat and draw out long strands of mucus, winding it around his finger as if he were curling up the string on a top. All her life, Mama loved hearing about her daddy sitting there at her side. It was one of the few times he had shown her the attention she craved from him. She often said her father's heart and mind had been as closed to her as a sealed book.

I knew my grandfather only from photographs. Jimmy Tucker was a good-looking man with a broad forehead and thick, curving lips. With his white linen summer suits and his racehorse named "Senator," he cut a romantic Southern figure, but he gambled and drank, and drink would be his downfall. He died of liver cirrhosis when Mama was a student at James Madison College.

Was his addiction part of the reason Mama always said her father "didn't know what to do with children?" Was it the reason they ate their meals in silence and he refused to have a Christmas tree? Whatever the reason, I found in looking through Mama's journals after she died that she was still trying to piece together clues to decipher her father's remote personality.

Her mother's family, on the other hand, was a high-spirited clan of seven sisters and three brothers. Most were socially active and pillars of their community. The "Cary women" were a tour de force and devoted to family. My childhood is filled with memories of family reunions and visits to my great aunts with their deep bosoms, moral admonitions and colorful life stories.

Dallas, Mama's mother, had a long graceful neck and rich folds of chestnut hair. She was extremely resourceful and a bit of a spitfire. Once she had slapped a teacher's face when she thought the teacher punished one of her sisters unfairly. When Jimmy's death left her with debt, she moved out of the large home he had built for her and rented it. She sold produce from her garden and supported her small family sewing beautiful clothing for the affluent women of her town.

Luckily for Mama, though her father was distant, her maternal grandfather doted on his first grandchild. He was warm and fun-loving—a tall rangy fellow with a full set of whiskers and an aquiline nose. He allowed her to help him in his blacksmith and wheelwright shops where she sorted nails and other bits of metal and put them into separate bins.

Toward hot summer's end, she went down through the fields with her grandfather to the watermelon patch. He taught her to look for the dried-up stem close to the melon, check for an even shape and a deep green stripe. He explained that if the stripes were running into one another, that meant the melon was over-ripe, "going toward rotten." They would rap on the green hide with their knuckles. If the sound was hollow, they had their melon. Then he pulled the fruit and gave it to her to carry. When they neared the house, he always said, "Now, stump your toe." She pretended to stumble and the melon tumbled to the ground and burst with a pop.

Then the two of them sat on the ground, pulling out the thick, red heart and eating it while the sweet juice ran down their arms. They dropped the rest of the melon and rind into the pigpen as they sauntered on back to the blacksmith shop, happy and satisfied with their secret.

These people and places were among the last to leave Mama's mind during our ride aboard the elephant.

Denial

The Elephant ride really began one fall morning in 1995. I arrived at Mama and Daddy's after dropping my daughter, Larkin, off at school. Larkin was twelve, awash in the excitement and uncertainties of middle school. Her steady and dependable nature was a bit bamboozled by the fray, and it was good to experience the stability of my parents' home after feeling my worries follow the small figure into the large school building.

The earthy smell of the leaves Daddy had heaped at the curb greeted me as I stepped from the car in front of their red-trimmed ranch house. I was glad Daddy, at eighty-five, was still able to rake his own leaves. His physical strength and robust love of life were cornerstones.

I always loved opening the red screen door on their carport, because I knew what lay behind it: coffee, laughter, and two people who had an undying interest in the minutiae of my life—a hard combination to beat. That morning, I expected to sink down on the blue couch with my steaming cup of coffee while they pushed back in their Lazyboys and we worked over the latest news, both global and family. If there were a dearth of subjects, we would trot out the old family stories and commiserate or laugh until our ribs ached.

As a freelance photographer, I made my own schedule and that always included time with my parents. My husband, Richard, was an engineering professor at Virginia Tech, where my father taught agronomy before he retired. Daddy had been a soil specialist, one of the people who created the first soil maps of Virginia by actually walking over miles of mountain, field and swamp, digging down with his auger and drawing out the soil for identification. After his retirement, he began painting landscapes. His work depicts farming, nature and wildlife, all things he loved. One scene hanging on my wall features a line of small sheep, looking somewhat like cutouts, heading toward an old-fashioned barn in a snow-covered field. In another scene, cattle stand in an iron blue creek while fish jump up underneath them to catch the insects flying around their bellies.

As I opened the door, I guessed we'd have a critique session on last week's painting: two wild turkeys walking a trail against a mountainside rich with fall color. I also expected, as this morning was Wednesday, that we would go over the grocery list Mama had prepared and I would shop for their weekly groceries. I had been their designated driver for the last two years.

When I walked in I could tell something was different. For one thing, there was no coffee aroma to greet me. For another, I could hear an unusual sound—my parents arguing as they came down the hall.

"Just let me see it again." Daddy's voice held a frantic note.

"No, Hobart. Don't scream in my ear. I'll give it to Diane when she comes. I've always done the checkbook. You don't know a thing about dealing with money."

Their accents reflected the Virginia locales where they had been born and raised. Mama's Southside drawl that pronounced the word "ear" as "eah" always conflicted with Daddy's mountain pronunciation of the word that sounded more like "err."

They bustled into the room—Mama, a small woman in a green apron, holding her checkbook up in the air away from Daddy, who was right behind her, shaking his head and frowning. They both looked relieved to see me. "Oh, Diane, I'm glad you're here. Come help me with this. Your father's upset because I've made some mistakes in these records." She went to the dining room table and sat. Behind her Daddy was gesticulating and mouthing words to me I couldn't understand. I pulled him into the kitchen.

"Get the checkbook away from her!" he whispered. "She's made all kinds of mistakes. Looks like chicken scratchins. I'm really worried."

I went and sat beside Mama. When she showed me the checkbook ledger, my heart sank. It looked like a child had been scribbling in it. Numbers and half words were written in random places and some of the marks made no more sense than, as Daddy said, chickens might make when they're picking at dirt in a hen yard.

I flipped the ledger back to the previous page. It looked normal. Some names of businesses were abbreviated, but the numbers were lined up and the decimals were all in the right places.

I turned back to the disorderly page. "When did you do this page, Mama?" I tried to make the words come out casually past the tightness in my throat.

"Last night, after your father went to bed, I was trying to reconcile with the bank statement. I know it's messy, but I was tired and the bulb in the lamp had gone out. I was too tired to change it." She leaned close to me. "You know how OLD I'm getting." She laughed. Mama loved to play the "old card." When telemarketers called, she demurred with, "I'm eighty-six. I'm too old to listen to you," and hung up the phone with a flourish. More and more she said, "Diane, you do up the dishes. I'm feeling too old."

My mind was grappling. Did Mama know something was wrong and was trying to cover it up, or was the page this way because of low light and tired eyes?

"Mama," I blurted out, "where's the coffee?"

She got to her feet and rolled her eyes toward Daddy. "Hobart's been carrying on so about the checkbook that we haven't even eaten breakfast. I'll fix some right now. Have you eaten?"

"Yes, but coffee would be great." I had another thought. "Where's the grocery list, Mama?"

"I haven't made it yet." She said airily, "I thought we could make it together." She went into the kitchen.

As soon as she was out of earshot, Daddy and I went into a huddle on the couch.

"Do you think something is really wrong? What else has she been doing"?

"Well, she forgets more things, names of things especially. But then so do I. But when I saw the checkbook…" He shook his head. "You know she's always been right on top of the money situation."

"Well, she said she was tired and the light bulb burned out."

"She didn't tell me that. She just got mad." He grinned for a moment. "Put me in my box."

Mama didn't get mad often, but when she did there was no crossing her. My parents hardly ever argued. Daddy had learned when to back up, shut up and take it. He called it "getting in his box" after his habit of telling his hunting dogs, when they barked too long, to "shut up and get in your box."

We sat there for a minute. Then I said, "OK, after breakfast, I'll get her to write out the grocery list. We'll see if she can do that. You go check that light bulb."

"Coffee's almost ready," Mama sang out from the kitchen.

The bulb was burned out. Mama insisted I write out the grocery list, but she remembered everything they needed to buy. But I wasn't satisfied. I had an uneasy feeling in my stomach, something I had learned to pay attention to. On the way to the store, I pulled the car over and examined the check she had given me for the groceries, signed as it always was. Her signature seemed perfectly normal. The "P" starting "Porter" was fat and pillow-like as usual. The writing wasn't shaky or spidery as often happens with elders' script as they start to falter.

As soon as I came back and the groceries were put away, I took the bank statement and reconciled her checkbook. Mama was pushed back in her Lazyboy when I took the ledger to her. Daddy had gone down to his art room in the basement to work on a painting. Instead of taking the ledger, she held her hand out in a "stop" motion. "Sit down, Diane. I've decided I want you to take over our money matters."

I dropped onto the couch. "What?" was the only word I could get out.

"It's just like when I decided to give up driving. I'd made some mistakes and I didn't want to hurt someone. Remember when they changed Main Street into four lanes and I went up the wrong side and had to drive right over that median strip?" She smiled and took a sip from her coffee cup on the end table. "Now, I don't want to lose any of the money I've saved, and I don't want..." she dropped her voice to a whisper and leaned toward me, "...Hobart to take it over. He knows nothing about money and cares less." She resumed a normal voice. "Do you remember what his mother said to me the day we told them we were engaged?"

I knew the story well, but wanted to see if she remembered it. "Well, I sort of remember…"

"His mother pulled me aside and asked me if I ever wanted to own my own house. I said I did and she said, 'Well, get Hobart's purse strings and keep them. He's generous and gullible to a fault about money. He'll give it away to anyone who asks him for it and you'll never have a cent.' Well, I did what she said. I've saved one hundred thousand dollars for our old age and we own this house." She settled deeper in her chair. "Now, I'm beginning to make a few little mistakes, and I want to give the money matters over to you, just like the driving. We'll have to go to the bank next week to sign some papers." She put her head back and closed her eyes as though the subject were closed.

I sat there, not knowing what to think. What she said made sense. She remembered the story perfectly. She seemed totally normal. But I remembered how my sister and I often said Mama was "foxy." She was a student of human nature and had her wiles and ways. She had told us about our children, "Don't let them get the upper hand." And about husbands, "A good time to ask them for something that you want is after sex." I studied her face. It was completely relaxed. Mama had always been the boss and I realized I didn't want that to change.

When I got home, I went straight to the phone and dialed my sister's number. It was one of the many times I lamented the fact that Beverly had moved away from these Virginia mountains. Bev and Mama were happily aligned in the traditions of hearth and home. Both their homes were places of comfort and organization where something homemade and delicious was always coming out of the oven. Their homes were orderly, Bev's three children were secure, and her husband's shirts were always pressed. I was the daughter with the unusual ideas and the crazy aunt that took Bev's children on escapades in the woods. I let pots burn and clothes mold in the washing machine while I pursued creative projects and played elaborate "pretend games" with my daughter.

Bev was also the champion and critic of my artistic endeavors. When I was in seventh grade and she was a high school sophomore, I wrote my first poem. I gave it to her to read right before I went to take a bath. About ten minutes later, she burst into the bathroom where I was soaking in the tub, pointed her finger at me and said, "You are a writer!" She then held the paper in front of me and began to point out the misspellings. "And there are only three things wrong with this poem."

"Three things wrong" became our joke, and later in life she used her knowledge as an English teacher to continue to critique my work. When her husband secured an important job with the University of Georgia, I knew how fractured the family would feel without the constancy of her role in our lives. I had wondered if I would have to stop taking photographs and start filing recipes to fill up the hole she would leave behind.

When her family left on moving day, Mama and Daddy rode down to Georgia with them to help with the children. I remember standing in the road with four-year-old Larkin in my arms, crying as they drove away. The children's hands waved from the back window like tiny rotating stars as they headed off to their new life.

"Giving up her checkbook?" Bev was incredulous. "That doesn't sound like Mama."

"Well, once she explained it, it did make sense. But how has she seemed on the phone to you? Have you noticed anything? Does she seem at all different?"

"Well, Mama is more forgetful, and sometimes she'll ask the same things over, but most older people do that." Bev was silent for a moment. "You know, maybe she can't see as well because of that cataract operation she had. Is it time for an eye check up?"

"Hmmm. That's a thought. Her eye appointment's next month. She just went to her regular doctor, and he didn't find a problem with anything. She does seem more tired, though."

"Well, they're both in their eighties. They're bound to be slowing down and more forgetful too. I think they do an awful lot for their age. Mama still cooks every day." Bev's tone began to lighten.

I joined right in. "And she does laundry and straightens up the house. You're right. They still do a lot. And it seems like all older people get peculiar about money. Remember when Grandma lived with us and she'd be hunting all over for her money and all the time it would be pinned in her bra?"

Bev laughed. "And she'd forget she'd taken her Ex-Lax and take it again and again. Maybe Mama just has a little hardening of the arteries like Grandma."

I felt calmer. "I think that's it. We have to face the fact that they're going to go through some changes. Nothing really to worry about."

"Well, I'll call Mama tonight and ask her some hard questions and call you and tell you how she seems. Let's not get all worked up for nothing."

"OK, let's not worry. I'm going to call Daddy and tell him not to worry."

Like the proverbial lemmings, we had rushed over the cliffs of doubt and thrown ourselves into the sea of denial. And once that path to the cliffs was mapped out, we continued to wear a groove in it. Every time doubt arose, we talked ourselves out of it. When Mama was diagnosed with hiatal hernia and reported to us that it was fatal, we said she must not have heard the doctor correctly. "He does mumble, sometimes." When she visited Georgia and told Bev's children she didn't love them, we comforted them with "She didn't really mean that. Three kids are just too much for an eighty-six year old. She was worn out." We continued trekking down that path into that comforting sea for several months until, suddenly, Daddy died.

Loss

When I think of what I know of my parents' life together, I think of two photographs that now sit in my dining room. One was taken toward the beginning of their courtship, the other toward the end of Daddy's life. Both are in black and white. In the first, they are standing beside a light-colored Model T Ford, both facing the camera. My father, virile as any Marlboro Man, stands with his legs apart, one outstretched arm braced against the car, his six-foot-three athletic frame leaning slightly in. In the space between him and the car, my mother floats like a small graceful ship tucked into a safe harbor, her body curving toward his body. In the background, sunlight glints on water.

The water is part of the New River, curling around the small mill town of Fries, deep in the Virginia mountains. In 1928, Daddy worked there in the mill, pitching baseball for the Farm League in his off-hours. He had been raised on a prosperous farm in a nearby county and, like his paternal uncles, was a "mountain man." Besides playing every sport in high school, he and his brother spent hours in the woods, putting out trotlines in the creeks, hunting for meat and trapping for fur. He rode his favorite horse to school, often standing up in the saddle, racing with the other boys.

My mother was beautiful but didn't know it. She was a slip of a woman, five foot two and ninety-eight pounds. But inside the slender body was a steady heart and strong backbone. She was raised on a farm, but loved to read so much that she taught herself to churn with her foot, so she could turn the pages of a book with her hands while she worked. Studious and shy with boys, after college she had come by train to Fries from her home in the Piedmont to get a job teaching school. Her father had died and the money she made would help support her mother and send her younger brother to college.

She met my father the day she arrived. They were both on their way to dinner in the town's only boarding house. She was crossing the foyer in her teacher's outfit when he came striding in the front door in coveralls. Their eyes met and Daddy said but one word. He said "Howdy," hung up his cap on a peg, and turned toward the dining room. Inside his head, his mind announced, "That's the girl you're going to marry." In my mother's mind, the popular song, "Love in Bloom" began to flow. They were engaged within the year.

In the second photo, Mama and Daddy pose, side by side, in front of their garden. She has on her broad-brimmed straw hat; he wears a pith helmet. They are both eighty-three and looking a little crepey around the edges, as though something in their bodies has deflated and left a space for their skin to sag into. But their smiles are full of light and their arms are bursting with produce: eggplant, squash, lush tomatoes. Behind them a stand of corn pushes plump tassels high into the air.

 Daddy would have loved to raise two healthy boys and pass on his farming and mountain wisdom, but his lot was daughters and he never complained. He took us girls into the fields and woods. I can see my sister now, at eight years old, driving our big red tractor across the field with Daddy standing behind on the plow, singing praise in her ear.

He taught us the names of plants and the habits of animals. We learned the tracks and scat of different creatures. We knew how to find owl-roosting trees by discovering the dry, gray "owl pellets" under the tree. These were oblong, fibrous balls of regurgitated matter that the owls couldn't digest from their meals of small rodents. I loved to pull the pellets apart with my fingers. The white color of tiny bones and teeth shining in the mass of rough hair seemed like the most magic of forest secrets.

In the fall we chewed "rabbit tobacco." We stripped the dry, leathery leaves from the stem of the everlasting plant, wadded them up and stuck them in our jaw, chewing until a spicy, deep-flavored liquid began to fill our mouths. Then we spat, not in the dribbly way of girls, but straight and far, pursing our lips and using our tongues the way Daddy taught us.

Daddy loved to watch red-tailed hawks. He trained us to identify them by their shape and red tail feathers as they floated above us on warm air thermals. We learned that they often traveled in pairs, male and female together. He said that in Indian lore the red-tailed hawks were considered messengers from other worlds.

Daddy always said he wanted to die in the woods, sitting under a tree. Instead he died sitting in the basement, feeding kindling into the woodstove that heated his art room. My uncle called it "the deluxe death"—healthy one minute, gone the next. Difficult for those left behind.

I had eaten lunch with them that day, the first day of March. Mama and I had prepared boiled shrimp with cocktail sauce, still a bit of an exotic treat for our small mountain town. After we ate, we studied over the Seed Catalogue for a while, making a list for spring planting. Then I hugged Mama and kissed Daddy on his bald spot, told them I loved them and went to deliver some photos to a client before picking up Larkin from school. She and I stopped on the way home to get some last-minute dinner items.

When we got home there were two messages on my machine. Both reported an ambulance and police cars in front of my parents' house. Larkin and I ran to the car. "Mom, your seat belt!" she cried as I broke speed limits and took corners on two wheels, making the fifteen-minute trip in record time.

We rushed past the emergency vehicles and burst in the door. Mama was in her Lazyboy, sitting upright, staring straight ahead. On either side of her stood a couple who were her neighbors, looking helpless. I kneeled beside her chair and she turned her head toward me. "Diane, your father is dead." I tried to embrace her, but she was like stone. "Go down to the basement and tell him goodbye," she intoned with no emotion.

I turned to Larkin who stood close with a pale face. "Do you want to come with me?"

"Should I?" Her voice was tiny. Her small hands on the ends of her long, slender arms worked against each other, over and over. I hesitated, not knowing what would be best. I turned to Mama, but she was still staring straight ahead. I wanted to embrace Mama, to reach out and pull my daughter close, but it seemed as though some invisible force was holding us in our separate places.

Finally I touched Larkin's arm. "Come on." I started for the stairs.

At the bottom of the basement steps, two men stood as though waiting for us. One wore a policeman's uniform, the other everyday clothes. They both glanced at us then looked at the floor, their hands clasped in front of them. The policeman nodded. "He's over there, ma'am."

They had stretched out Daddy's body on the spare bed. The minute I saw him I knew that the vibrant, life-loving spirit was absent, was absolutely gone. The body lay on its back, the knees slightly bent, the head thrown back at a strange angle. The eyes were closed, the mouth open as though the spirit had perhaps flown from there. The skin was already tinged with gray.

But even though I knew he was gone, even though strangers and my own daughter watched me, when I saw the familiar square shape of his hands, the blunt nails that I often trimmed, the white curl of hair behind his ear, I wanted to crawl onto the bed and gather my father's great body up in my arms. I wanted to lay my cheek against his cheek and breathe in his familiar smell and whisper, "Please, please, not yet. Please don't leave us yet."

Instead I silently reached out and touched his face. To my surprise it was quite warm. I swung around to the standing men. "He's still warm! Are you sure he's dead?"

The policeman took a step toward me. "The wood stove, ma'am. He was sitting in front of it. That's why he's warm."

"What was it? What killed him?" I realized I didn't even know.

"Heart attack, ma'am. Sudden. He probably didn't suffer." Neither man looked me in the eye.

Larkin stood staring at her grandfather's body, both arms clutched tight around herself. When I asked if she wanted to touch him she shrank back, crying out, "No!" in a stricken voice.

I quickly took her back up the stairs. With each step, my body seemed heavier, my head more hot and tight. I wanted to say the right thing, to do something to help my daughter, to help my mother, but instead something big and heavy seemed to be growing inside me, taking me over. *If I could just have a moment, just a moment to collect myself.* I headed for the bathroom and splashed cold water on my face. When I raised my head to the mirror, Larkin was reflected there, staring at me, her eyes huge. I looked from her to me. I was shocked to see I looked the same as I had that morning. How could I look the same when so much had changed, when this enormous thing was crowding me, stretching my insides to the splitting point? I sat down on the edge of the tub and took some deep breaths.

Larkin peered at me anxiously, her arms still wrapped around her body. "What do we do now?" she whispered.

I wanted to answer, "We break. We break to pieces and fall down and cry." But the pleading look in her eyes kept me from saying that. She needed me to set her world back in place. She was taking her cues from me.

It was a moment when my larger self called on my smaller self. I took a deep breath. The feeling pressing inside me would have to wait. I took her hands, looked into her eyes and said calmly, "We do what needs to be done. We call Aunt Bev. We take care of Grandma. Death is a part of life and life goes on." Relief softened her face and her shoulders relaxed. A grownup was still in charge. I pulled her against me and found solace in my daughter's warmth.

Back in the living room, the neighbors were still hovering and Mama was still silent and staring. I took the neighbors' arms and thanked them for coming over. Their story tumbled out. How Mama came down through their adjoining yards, burst in on them and told them about Daddy, how they had come back with her, found my father in the basement and called 911.

While they were talking, Mama suddenly got up and headed for the kitchen. "I never did eat my supper." She spoke as though talking to herself. We looked at one another, and then the four of us followed her. The round yellow kitchen table was set for two, the food, now cold, already dished up on the white and blue plates—a salad of lettuce and canned pears topped with blue cheese dressing, a helping of casserole made from the leftover shrimp, a slice of Roman Meal bread, water in glasses sweating where the ice had melted.

She sat down at her place at the table, put her paper napkin in her lap and began to eat, seemingly oblivious to our presence. We stood behind her in a semi-circle, a mute tableau, watching her methodically lift the fork, use the napkin. The only sounds were the clink of her silverware on the plate, the sound of our breathing. The smell of shrimp rose into the air. Outside the window a redbird flitted past on its way to the feeder. She raised her glass and drank, set it back down. Larkin hung onto my arm. I knew I should do something or say something, but I didn't know what.

Then one neighbor looked at me and mouthed the words, "She's in shock."

The words released me into action. I ushered the neighbors out, thanking them and asking them to call the other neighbors and give them the news. I heard the outside basement door open and I knew the men were taking the body out to the ambulance. They would have to pass the kitchen window. "Mama, we need to go in the living room now." I led her to her Lazyboy. She was still clutching her fork in one hand. Larkin stayed right beside us, taking it all in.

I drew a straight back chair up beside Mama. "Mama, tell me what happened. Tell me how Daddy died." She looked right at me then and I saw reality come flooding into her face. The fork fell to the floor. Her lips began to tremble and her eyes bore into mine. "Diane!" she said. Tears flooded her eyes but didn't fall. I watched Mama struggle for composure and win. In all the crises of our lives I had seen her cry only twice. It seemed as though breaking down was a luxury that she would not, or could not allow herself.

In a strained voice, she told us the story. "Hobart had gone down to his painting room earlier and I had fixed supper. I called him, but he didn't answer, so I thought he had gone outdoors. I went out, and couldn't find him, so I came in through the basement and..." She stopped for a moment and brought her hand to her eyes. "He was sitting in front of the wood stove, slouched over to one side. At first I thought he had fallen asleep, but when I touched his hand, I knew. I sat there with him..." Now a few tears did slip down. "...and told him goodbye." She took a deep breath. "I tried to call you or Richard, but couldn't get you, so I went down to the neighbors and they helped me with everything." She wiped her eyes. "I called Beverly and she's probably already on her way."

There was a knock on the front door. The Policemen said they were taking the body to the funeral home. When I turned back to Mama she was sitting up with dry eyes, saying to Larkin, "We'd better straighten up the house. People will be coming."

People came: Beverly and her family, other relatives and friends, my father's colleagues. They started coming that evening and kept coming for days, before and after the funeral, bearing pots of hearty soup, beautiful fruit salads, ham biscuits and casseroles, stories of my father, memories, hugs and tears, sometimes laughter, sometimes awkward silences which seemed to be just as healing as everything else. Cards poured in, the doorbell rang with flower deliveries. The community was circling one of its own.

Grief

Throughout the flutter of activity, I stayed focused on Mama. She seemed to be in another world at times, at times very present—with us, then far away. But that seemed a somewhat normal response. We all felt a bit that way. She did do some odd things. She refused to wear "church shoes" to the funeral. Instead she insisted on wearing an old pair of white tennis shoes. At the graveside she sat in the car for most of the service. Once, when someone came to the house to offer condolences, she completely ignored her, working furiously with a cloth trying to get a stain out of one of her chairs while Bev talked to the visitor. When we asked her about it, she frowned then said airily, "I've never liked her. I don't know why she had to come." We let it go.

I knew my attention to Mama also helped me quell that pressing feeling inside me that grew, receded, and then grew again. The day after the funeral, I was alone at my house for the first time since Daddy died. While I sat exhausted on the couch, my gray cat jumped up and sleekly ambled over to settle herself in my lap. Not unusual for a cat, except this one had never sat on anyone's lap and hardly liked to be petted.

"Grief must have a smell," I whispered to the cat. That started the waves inside me rolling. I grabbed a jacket and took off down through the fields toward Shadow Lake, a small green pond set in a circle of woods.

As the March wind lifted the smell of earth, a wave of loss rose inside me. The slip of weeds against my legs, a birdcall from the forest's edge, the clouds pushing across the blue sky—everything reminded me of Daddy. When I neared the lake and saw the emerald water shimmer between the trees, I began to run. With each jolting step, huge chunks of grief broke loose inside me. Branches slapped my face and chest as I tore through the trees and stumbled into the open space beside the lake. By the time I reached the bank I was howling. I lay there with my head on the new spring grass and gave myself over to the tide.

That night I felt lighter and freer than I had in days. One of my nieces and my nephew were coming to spend the night, and Larkin and I set the table with paper plates for pizza. I mused on our customs around death, our way of dealing with loss in mainstream America, the unspoken rise of sorrow that we feel we can't express except privately.

I had read of South American countries where people ran into the street wailing after someone died. The neighbors joined in, holding the person and grieving with them. I had heard about women in India keening and smashing down their arms in grief to break their glass bracelets and cut themselves. I understood how causing yourself physical pain could somehow alleviate or at least reflect the pain you felt inside. These more public methods of grieving seemed healthier to me than our choked back emotions, how we surreptitiously dabbed at our eyes with Kleenex, pressing the grief back inside our bodies, how I had taken my grief to nature rather than the community of people.

I watched my daughter as she set out forks and napkins. Except for her light brown hair to his dark, she looked like her dad. She had his well-drawn features, soulful brown eyes, and slender form. We named her Larkin because when Richard and I were just hanging out

at home, having fun together, we said we were "larkin'."
She had those light qualities, but there was also a deep
and steady river that ran through her nature and she
often kept these deeper waters private. She reminded me
of Mama in many ways. I had not seen her weep for her
grandfather. Would she carry this sadness with her into
her later years? Was I amiss not to wail and cry with her,
give her permission to grieve openly?

I also wondered about Mama, who seemed to have no
outward methods of relieving herself from her sadness.
Did she cry during the night when she was alone? Did
she ever beat, or thrash, or wail? I remembered the
stories of how she was silenced as a child by the very
presence of her enigmatic father. There was no talking at
mealtime.

"Be quiet! Your Daddy's coming," her mother would
say when he came home from work. Although he forbade
having a Christmas tree, Mama would give him gifts and
instead of opening them he put them away in a drawer.
She went to check the drawer every week. For months the
presents lay there, still wrapped in the paper she had so
carefully chosen. Then one day they would be gone, but
even if she saw him wearing the pair of socks, or using the
handkerchiefs that she had given him, he never spoke of
them.

Was that why we enjoyed the towering Christmas
trees of my childhood, their tops brushing the ceiling,
elegantly festooned with the beautiful glass balls and the
delicate painted metal birds that Mama treasured? One
year we thought Beverly was allergic to evergreens, so
Mama had Daddy cut a regular bare-branched tree from
the woods, and we painstakingly covered every limb and
twig with tinfoil before decorating it with all the usual
ornaments.

My thoughts were interrupted as two of my sister's kids came in, Sarah and "Little" Ed. The children had tired of the wonderful food from neighbors and friends and were looking forward to pepperoni pizza. It was good and it was easy. It felt like balm to have my sister's children with us on the night after Daddy's funeral.

When the curly-headed Sarah, now eighteen, had been born, she had the largest, most luminous blue eyes I had ever seen. Daddy and I couldn't seem to stay away from the hospital. We'd be on our way to the grocery store and all of a sudden I'd make a sharp turn off our route.

Daddy would laugh, "Going to the hospital?"

"Yep. I just realized it's viewing time."

"Let's go then!"

Sarah had kept her luminous beauty and loved old-fashioned ways. Although she loved to laugh and dance, she seemed to belong to another time when women had strong morals and gentle manners, rooted in home and family. She often said she had been born in the wrong era.

Ed, called "Little Ed" because he was the third of three Edwards, was celebrated for being the only boy of children or grandchildren. Daddy had poured all his male mentoring into Ed, teaching him sports, taking him fishing, going to his ball games in Georgia during our many visits. Since Daddy was too old and Ed too young to actually go hunting, they would go down in the basement and make up pretend duck blinds with old blankets. They practiced shooting pretend guns when pretend ducks flew overhead. If you asked Ed today if he had ever gone duck hunting, he would probably say "yes."

All our children had loved to go to Mama and Daddy's house. When they lived in the same town, Bev's two girls had taken their little suitcases and gone together to spend the night. They were allowed to stay up late and eat as much honey bread as they wanted. Visiting from Georgia, they would take over the basement. With Larkin as the smallest member of the clan, they all played pretend games as long as we adults would let them stay up.

The pizza arrived. We sat around my dining room table and I lit the group of large white and tan candles in the middle. Two of Daddy's paintings hung on the walls around us. He often painted from photographs that he or I had taken, and the smaller piece was from one of my photos. In it, a long line of trees beside a fencerow threw their deep blue shadows across a snowy field, while sunset clouds marched across the sky. The larger one was rich with the pink and green colors of spring. Chartreuse trees just leafing out and pink redbuds dotted the small gentle mounds called Peddler Hills.

Richard and the children and I chatted and gossiped in a halfhearted way about the relatives and friends whom we had seen that day. The pizza gave out and Richard excused himself and went upstairs. The children and I still sat there, our voices gradually ceasing as the light coming in the windows dimmed into darkness. We all gazed at the steadily burning candlelight, breathed in the thick smell of unscented wax. I had put on a CD of Native American music and it swelled into the silence— Indian drums and flutes and the long call of a wolf. Although we didn't speak, there was no discomfort. We were very much together.

Then, at the same moment, two of the larger candles overflowed and spilled wax into big pools on the wooden table. No one moved to clean up the wax. Instead we sat silently staring, our faces glazed into radiant masks by the gentle light. After the pools cooled a bit, I took my dinner knife and slowly scraped one up in a soft, flat piece. "I love to play with warm wax," I mused and began to squish and shape the wax in my hands.

Sarah pried up the other pool and soon we were all quietly playing with the heated wax. We poured it onto our paper plates from the candle wells, dipped our fingers in it, and pinched off the soft tops of the candles next to the flames. We squeezed and worked it into shapes, then held the shapes to the flames to soften them again. Once in a while, one of us would show a shape to the others, then return to our silent absorption.

I wondered absently if we were ruining my table, but I couldn't seem to care. As the darkness deepened, the candlelight appeared brighter. The music curled around us: the sounds of creeks running, hawks calling and mournful chants that spoke of loss and longing and magic. From the sideboard, Mama and Daddy watched us from their photographs.

When I think back on that scene, I feel we were engaged in some unspoken ritual of grief and healing, a family passage that would hold us together like wax, now that one of the elders had left us. The next morning, I got up and scraped the table. I wrapped one flat chunk of wax in a pretty piece of cloth and put it a drawer where I keep lifelong treasures.

Aftermath

Then, suddenly, the others had gone back to their regular lives and it was just Mama and I at her house. After all the people, the hubbub and the distractions were over, after life returned to normal, I began to realize that "normal life" for us had been disrupted forever. Finding a new sense of normalcy was hard and sad work. I stayed with Mama at her house for about two weeks. We clung to the old routines. We cooked and took walks. She went with me to the grocery store, to pick Larkin up, and to my house to do chores. We planned the garden, just tomatoes and cucumbers this year. We read the sympathy cards that still came, entertained the occasional visitor. Sometimes I cried. Mama didn't, but often she seemed as though she moved in a fog.

We all missed Daddy. In Georgia, right after Daddy died, Sarah was in their basement working at a computer in front of a window when a red-tailed hawk flew down and looked in at her intently. Sarah had the strong feeling that the hawk was her grandfather watching over her. She wrote a poem about the experience, but didn't tell anyone until much later. When Rachel spent time with Mama in the next year, she told us later that at night she sometimes went to the cemetery and lay on her grandfather's grave. I found a note written by Larkin. "My grandfather died today. He was the best man I know."

Even poetry failed Mama and me. We had always read poetry aloud to one another, but when I tried to soothe us with readings, there were too many poems that spoke of sadness and death. "Not that," she'd say to Frost's "Stopping by Woods on a Snowy Evening."

"I can't hear that now." she declared when I tried to read "The Ballad of the Harp Weaver" by Millay. She wasn't even comforted by "Sailing to Byzantium," a poem she loved so well that I had copied her favorite verses in calligraphy for her birthday.

One night during the second week, from my bed in the spare room, I heard her slippers clop up the hall toward the living room. I got up as she was coming back down the hall, huddled deep in her pink bathrobe in the dim night-light. She stopped when she saw me and fixed me with an anxious stare. "Are you kin to me?" she whispered.

I flipped on the light. "Mama! It's me, Diane. What are you doing up?"

She peered at me and blinked. "Water," was all she said.

I got her some water and decided to sleep in her bed, regardless of her snoring. I thought she must have been half-asleep or dreaming to ask who I was. Nothing to worry about.

The next morning she seemed fine. It was a chilly spring morning so I got up to cut on the heat, and then snuggled back in with her until the house warmed up. We began to feel our stomachs, and talk about them and the food we had eaten the night before.

"Mine feels like a fat little roast hen," she exclaimed.

"Let me feel it." I smoothed her little tummy under her blue flowered pajamas. "No it's much smaller. Let's see...maybe a Cornish hen."

"Really? That small? How about a pullet?"

"Maybe a capon?" I asked.

She chuckled and slapped both hands on her stomach. "A capon? A capon is larger than a pullet. You weren't raised with chickens to take care of like I was!"

"Well, then I know what it is. It's a quail!"

"I wish I had some quail to fry for our breakfast," she said quietly. We were still a moment. I knew we were both thinking of how Daddy would bring a brace of quail in from his hunt. He'd let me feel their downy feathers, and I was fascinated by the way their heads lolled so loosely on their necks. He sat by the heating duct in the kitchen with a paper bag between his knees to pick the birds. I liked to sit near and smell the warm animal odor that came from them. Sometimes he pulled out their crops and smashed open the small, delicate sack with his thumb to show me the contents. It was always filled with different colors and sizes of seeds. He would talk about how we could tell where the birds had been by what they ate. After he finished cleaning the birds, Mama soaked them in salt water and soon we'd be eating them fried up crisp and crunchy for our meal.

"Let me feel your stomach." She rolled towards me and rubbed my belly. "Hmmm..."

"What, Mama, what does it feel like?"

"A turkey." She giggled. "Stuffed!" We laughed. Mama and I always had fun together, even over the silliest things. Once she had even dubbed me "the fun child," and in return, I called their house "my laughing place."

I hated to leave her when she finally insisted that I go back to my house, but I knew it was probably for the best. Life must go on. My family missed me and the bit of money I earned from my photography helped pay the bills. After all, we lived in the same town. I could drop by every day, and Bev had invited her to come down to Georgia soon for a nice long visit.

Things went well for about a month. Then one day when I walked in, the house was full of a thin, bluish smoke. Mama sat serenely in her Lazyboy reading the newspaper. "Mama, smoke! Go outside, quick." I ran to the kitchen. Smoke was pouring out from around the oven door. I threw it open and there sat a plastic Tupperware bowl melted into a distorted shape. What looked like a squash casserole was dripping down onto the floor of the oven. I grabbed a cookie sheet and potholders, slid the mess onto the cookie sheet, and then threw it out the back door into the grass. Mama was standing in the doorway to the kitchen. "I don't think I put that in my oven!"

That night I packed Mama's suitcase and moved her into the spare room at my house. After a few nights of "visiting," she was ready to go home. When I tried to explain things to her, she was both amazed and adamant. "Good heavenly days, Diane, I don't need anyone watching me! I want to go home!" I packed my suitcase and moved back to Mama's.

There were many calls to and from Georgia. Bev and I both got brochures on Alzheimer's disease from our doctors' offices. But from the description, Mama didn't have it. "If you forget *where* your keys are, that's normal aging. If you forget *what* your keys are for, that could be a sign of Alzheimer's." I gave her little tests. Mostly she passed them. I would pretend to forget the names of certain relatives as we perused family scrapbooks, or ask how many tomato plants we had set out. One day she stared at me over the top of her glasses. "Diane, you sure are forgetful for someone of your age."

We didn't know how to proceed. We only knew we didn't want her to be alone for any long periods of time. I prepared all the food or we did it together, but going from one household to the next was taking its toll on me. I began to turn down photo jobs, to back out of social engagements. Though they never said so, I figured my family was feeling my absence at home and I was missing them. It seemed almost like we were waiting for Mama to indicate what to do next. Then one Saturday, the second week I had been staying there, I went back to my house for a few hours and the phone rang. It was Mama's next-door neighbor, John. He said Mama had come to his door and asked him to help her find her way back home. The writing was on the wall. We had to get help.

Bev and I decided to hire a sitter. I knew there were people who sat with the elderly, just as baby sitters sat with kids. After asking around, I called the local retirement home and got a list of people who took sitting jobs. Bev and I decided that my niece, Rachel, who was studying at Washington and Lee University, just two hours away, could come down and help me find somebody appropriate for Mama.

There's Nobody Out There

Rachel was the first grandchild, greatly desired and deeply nurtured. I was living in Pennsylvania when she was born. When I came back to Blacksburg two weeks later, my sister met me at her front door, holding dainty Rachel up in a white blanket. Bev's face was foolish with love. "Look what I've got here!" was her greeting.

Rachel grew into a tall, beautiful young woman, with the grace and elegance of a lily. She had inherited her father's wicked wit and, like the rest of us, loved to laugh. Even as a small child, she had shown such presence and keen observation that Mama and Daddy said she would grow up to be a lawyer. They were right.

Mama was taking a nap and Rachel and I were sitting on the couch with two phones, two glasses of iced tea and the list of sitters. We were elated that the list was so long. Surely, from all these names, some of them would be perfect for Mama. Unbelievably, one of them even had the last name of Nightingale.

"This is either a sign from heaven or a gimmick," I said, as I happily dialed her number.

"Yes?" answered a deep female voice that sounded decidedly cross.

"Could I speak to Dreama Nightingale?"

"That's me. What is it?" The woman definitely sounded annoyed.

"Ah, do you have a moment to talk?"

"Yes." Still brusque. It must just be her way of talking.

Rachel and I exchanged frowns before I continued, "Well, I'm looking for a sitter for my mother. She's eighty-seven and recently lost her husband. She's in pretty good health, but has some dementia and needs some care—mostly just companionship and food preparation. I wondered what kinds of services you offer."

Her voice became very loud. "Well, I'll do anything. I've cared for all kinds of people and I know people with dementia need a firm hand." Her voice deepened and took on the cadence of a drill sergeant. "I get them up, dress them, bathe them, feed them, walk them, bed them down. I charge $10.50 an hour and I don't work weekends."

Rachel was rolling her eyes and shaking her head wildly.

I knew I would never let this woman anywhere near Mama, but I didn't quite know how to get off the phone. "Well, thank you. I'll talk to my sister and let you know if we need you."

"You won't get no better deal than this." Her voice now had a threatening quality to it.

"Well, yes, I'll keep that in mind." I hung up quickly.

Rachel and I stared at each other. "Well, I have a feeling that name didn't come down through a bloodline," Rachel commented dryly.

"Maybe that attitude is what got Florence through the war," I said.

"Well, she wouldn't last two minutes with Grandma." We both laughed.

Even in her condition, Mama was still the boss of her household. One thing she couldn't stand was what she called a "take-over person," especially in her own domain.

After two more calls with no answer I contacted an answering machine message that sounded so hostile that I quickly hung up. Rachel raised her eyebrows. "Another Nightingale, no doubt." We took long drinks of tea.

Thankfully, the next call reached a gentle-sounding woman who seemed perfect except for the fact that she was booked up for months. We asked her if she knew of someone else, but she said the best sitters were already working at the retirement center. We left our number with her, just in case.

I dialed the next number on the list. Lori was a college student and sounded flustered at my call. "Let's see...my classes have changed since I put my name on that list. Hold on a minute. OK, let's see. I could come two Saturdays from now, but only in the afternoon. I always sleep late on Saturday and there's a game that night...Hold on a sec. I could also come two weeks after that on the twenty-eighth, for a couple of hours in the morning. That's as far ahead as I can tell you now."

"Well, we were hoping for someone who could come on a more regular basis," I ventured.

"Oh, no. I couldn't possibly do that. I'm working on my thesis." She sounded amazed that I didn't understand how busy she was.

The next call was a woman named Millie who seemed eager to take the job. She had no car, but didn't live too far from town. I was making arrangements to meet with her when she said, "There's one other thing. Ellory will have to come with me most days, but he ain't no problem."

"Ellory?"

"Yes, he's my brother's boy. I watch him most days. But he ain't no problem. He just sits there, watchin' the TV."

"Oh...well..." I thought about how Mama loved children. Maybe this would work out for everyone. "How old is Ellory?"

"Oh, he's twenty-six or seven. Don't rightly know. But like I say, as long as he can watch the TV, he ain't no trouble."

Rachel was giving me the "thumbs down" sign.

"Well, I don't think that would work," I said. "Mama really doesn't like to keep the television on."

"Don't she sleep a lot?" Millie asked quickly.

"Excuse me?"

"Well, most old folks sleep a lot. He could watch the TV then."

"Well, no, no she doesn't sleep a lot, not really."

"Can't you put the TV in another room?"

Rachel suddenly spoke up from her phone, "No, Millie, we can't. We can't move the TV to another room. We're sorry. Goodbye."

We clicked off and exchanged looks. Rachel observed wryly, "Perhaps we should introduce Ellory to Dreama Nightingale. She'd get him up from in front of the TV, walk him, feed him, bed him down, and give poor Millie a break." We hooted with laughter.

Rachel unfolded her long body from the couch. "Before we call anyone else, we need treats!" I followed her, but before we reached the kitchen, the phone rang. We sat back down and lifted our phones. The voice on the other end of the phone was slow as pond water. "I hear you're needin' a sitter, an' I'd like to do it."

"Well, I'm glad you called... Who told you about us?"

"My cousin Ruby over to the retirement home." Wow, news travels fast.

"And your name is..."

"El-vira, Elvira Simms. I'd have to be paid in cash."

"Oh... I see. And why is that?"

"We don't truck with no tax people."

"Hmmm, well, Elvira, have you had much experience sitting for people?"

"Wa-l-l, no."

"Have you had any experience sitting with people?"

"My grandma, but she died on me."

Rachel was frantically gesturing for me to "cut it."

"I'm sorry Elvira. We're looking for someone more experienced. Goodbye."

"I think we're going to need more than treats to get us through this," Rachel stated flatly. "Let's get out the tequila and some salt."

I couldn't seem to summon up a laugh. "I'll settle for ice cream," I said and started to get up.

Immediately the phone rang again. We both picked up and a coarse male voice demanded, "You called my answerin' machine and hung up and I want to know who you are and why you're callin'!"

I was dumbfounded. "What?"

"My answerin' machine! You called it! I want to know why!" Then I realized this was the person with the rough sounding message I had hung up on. He must have caller ID.

"Well, I... I realized I had the wrong number when I heard your message, so I hung up," I faltered.

There was a suspicious silence at the other end of the phone. Then, "OK, but you better not call here again!" The phone was slammed down.

"What in the hell was that all about?" Rachel said with a look of amazement on her face. I could only shake my head. We both slumped back into the couch and sat there staring into space, treats forgotten. After a long moment Rachel moved over to me, put her arm around my shoulders and leaned close. The smell of her perfume was comforting. "Diane," she whispered in my ear, "there's nobody out there."

Found Sitters

There turned out to be someone out there—many someones. We had only touched the tip of the sitter iceberg. There would be sitters all along this elephant ride. The problem was getting one we could afford, and Mama would accept, and one who had a schedule compatible with our needs.

About two weeks after Rachel went back to school, I found someone I thought might work out. She was a short, boxy-looking woman named Carole with very close-cropped hair. She lived with an elderly relative and would be able to spend the weeknights with Mama, give her morning medicines and fix breakfast for them both. Then I would come and stay or take Mama with me, to my home or wherever else I was going that day.

Carole was a shy woman, who talked nervously about nothing. I had to warn her about seeming to be a "take-over person" in Mama's home. I told her she should go stay in her room if Mama seemed annoyed with her presence. She said she understood old people and their quirks and wouldn't take it personally.

I talked with Mama several times about the reasons Bev and I thought she needed someone to stay the nights with her, and she seemed agreeable, but not at all enthusiastic. She often didn't remember our conversations.

The introductions went well. Carole was not too talkative and Mama was pleasant enough, asking questions about her family and where she had lived. But when Carole went to put her suitcase in the spare bedroom Mama turned to me in surprise. "Why are you putting that little man in my house?"

"Mama," I whispered, "she's not a man. Carole is a woman. She's..."

"He looks like a man to me!" Mama peered down the hall toward the bedroom.

"Mama, I promise you that is a woman. Her hair is just very short. You know that's a style nowadays." I put my arm around her. "Remember, Beverly and I want you to have someone to stay with you at night. We don't want you to be here alone. But we certainly wouldn't hire a man."

"Hire?" Mama moved away from me. "You all are *paying* someone to stay here with me? Why, I used to stay here alone all the time when Hobart was teaching those extension classes!"

I could hear Carole coming up the hall. "Mama, please, just try this for a little while—so Bev and I won't worry."

"For goodness sake." Mama grumbled under her breath as she sat heavily in her chair.

After showing Carol around, I decided to exit fast and hope for the best. All evening I resisted the urge to call and went to bed worried.

The next morning before I was hardly dressed, the phone rang. "Diane?" It was Carole and she sounded distressed.

"Yes, Carole. What's going on?"

"Your mother...I tried to get her to take her pills and...and...she hit me!" Carole broke into sobs. "I didn't do anything to her, I swear. She just..."

"Carole, I'm so sorry. Where is Mama now?"

"She's in the living room. I'm on her bedroom phone with the door closed."

"Are you OK?"

"Yes, I just…"

"Please calm down. Don't do anything else! Just stay where you are until I get there. I'm on my way." As I ran out of the house, I called to Richard that he would have to take Larkin to school.

Mama was sitting in her Lazyboy with a regal air when I burst in the door. Carole was nowhere in sight. "Mama, are you all right? Where is Carole?"

Mama turned to me with outrage in her eyes. "I'm certainly glad you've come! Do you know what that little man did? He threw up in my kitchen sink, then he tried to force pills on me. I closed him up in the bedroom."

I knelt beside her chair. "You, Mama, are you alright?"

"Of course I am."

"Mama, did you, ah, hit the little man?"

Mama lost her regal air and looked confused. She gazed down at her lap and shook her head. Her voice became small. "I'm…I don't think I did. I was mad. He tried to force pills on me in my own home." She looked at me beseechingly. "He threw up in my sink—you know I can't stand anything like that." Her voice trailed off.

I found Carole sitting on Mama's bed clutching a Kleenex to her red eyes. There was a pile of used tissues on Mama's pillow.

"Carole, I'm so sorry. Tell me what happened." I sat beside her on the bed.

"Well, she was disoriented in the night and came and got in my bed with me. I took her back to her bed and then this morning I helped her dress and we ate breakfast, and then when I tried to give her the pills like you showed me, she got mad and started to hit on me."

"Did she hurt you?"

"Not really." Carole sniffed into her tissue. "I turned around so she mostly just hit my back, but it was just so surprising." Her eyes welled up. "I thought we were doing so good."

"I am so, so sorry. She's really never done anything like this before. It must be the dementia. I'm so glad she didn't really hurt you." I touched her arm. "And she said something about your throwing up in the kitchen sink?"

"Yeah, I must have a bug or something. I knew I couldn't make it to the bathroom." She wiped her nose and dropped the Kleenex onto the pile on the pillow.

Mama wouldn't speak to Carole, only glared at her as Carole left the house. When I went in the kitchen there was still vomit in the sink. After a short conversation, Bev and I decided the "little man" would have to go and I would have to lecture Mama on corporal punishment.

It took me a week to decide to try someone else. Mama had begun to wander in the night. From the spare room, I would hear the drag, clop, drag, clop of her slippers in the hall. When I went out to her, she was often disoriented, but sometimes just on her way to the bathroom, or to the kitchen for water. On the nights she asked me if I was kin to her, I got back in her bed, so tired that her snoring didn't bother me. I decided to put my photographic clients on hold. Mama was turning into a full time job.

I returned to the sitter list with a vengeance. After several interviews, I found someone with good references who seemed perfect. Her name was Lily and she and Mama liked each other right away, perhaps because Lily would never be mistaken for a man. Small and gentle with grayish curls that looked like they were put up at night with bobby pins, she joked about her retired husband being underfoot and seemed almost glad she'd be away for the weeknights. Lily offered to cook Mama's supper for her as well as breakfast and asked if she could read to Mama in the evenings.

I decided to be very involved and spent part of the first evenings with them, enjoying some of Lily's "good country food"—pork chops with biscuits, cooked apples and greens. After we ate, Lily read to us out of *Guidepost Magazine* and *The Ladies Home Journal*. We all enjoyed ourselves and I thought the extra money Lily charged was worth it. After two weeks of Lily, I began to relax. Then one day Lily called and said Mama was calling her names and barring her from the kitchen. I went over right away and tried to negotiate, but Mama was mad and adamant. She said she didn't need anyone under her feet, especially a "take-over person" like Lily had turned out to be. Lily left with hurt feelings and her suitcase.

In desperation, I hired a woman who had checked out my groceries at the supermarket for years. In chatting to her about my plight, I learned that Mildred was retiring the next week and would like to try sitting with the elderly for extra money. She seemed a good-hearted person so I told her we'd give it a try.

She didn't last even one evening. Mama blessed her out and Mildred called me. She was sitting in her car outside when I pulled up into Mama's driveway after her phone call.

"You got your hands full!" she said before she gunned her motor and drove off.

When I got in the house, Mama was watching TV and said she didn't remember anyone being there.

I called Bev and we arranged for Mama to make a nice long visit to Georgia. Soon after Mama got to Georgia, I began to question my sanity. Bev wasn't having any problems with Mama. Every time I called, things were fine. Mama was staying in her bed at night, was able to stay alone for short periods, and generally acting normal. I began to wonder if I had overreacted to Mama's problems. Had I made her worse by forcing strangers onto her? Perhaps the dementia had just been a response to Daddy's death. Maybe all Mama needed was a little vacation and when she returned she would be her old self again. Deep inside me, hope began to rise like helium in my bones.

Then one night Bev called late and said in a slurred voice, "Diane, I just drank a whole bottle of wine."

Dread axed its way through my body. My sister was not much of a drinker.

"Oh, no. What happened?" I asked.

"You know all the problems you'd been having with Mama?"

"Yes, what happened?"

"Well, I thought maybe it was jus' that you..." Her voice trailed off.

"Beverly, what has happened? Tell me."

There was a long pause, then, "She's been peeing."

"Peeing," I repeated. "What do you mean? Peeing in her bed?"

"Nope. In a shoe."

"What?"

"Wait. I gotta' get some water." She clunked down the phone and picked it up a few moments later. "O.K. Feel better now. Tell you the whole story. Mama knocked on my door about four in the morning a few nights ago. When I went out in the hall, she said she was afraid she'd done shome-thing, ah, something wrong. Diane, she looked so tiny and pitiful..." Bev's voice caught. Then she cleared her throat. "She took me to her room, and you know the walk-in closet where I keep extra clothes?"

"Of course, the one where Sarah used to play with her Barbies."

"Right. Well, Mama took me into the closet and showed me where she'd peed in one of Rachel's old shoes—a flat, black pump. Then I noticed an odor and saw where she had peed several times in the trash can that was in there. It was almost overflowing."

"Oh no!"

"She was so upset and embarrassed. You know how fashtid-fash-fash."

"Fastidious," I chime in.

"Right. Mama is so fash-tidious about such things. And Diane, then she asked me if I was kin to her. She didn't even know me!" Bev's voice speeded up. "Then yesterday I left her with the girls and they were talking about Daddy being gone and the girls told her that she wasn't alone, they loved her and were here for her, and she told them she didn't care about that and didn't love them."

Bev stopped and I heard her gulping more water. "The girls were so upset. You know Mama would never say anything like that. But when I came back she acted fine. It's just all so sad. Little Mama feeling alone, wandering around in the night, peeing in things, not even knowing how to find a toilet, not even knowing the people who love her."

Bev's voice broke and she took some long breaths. "And now I'm exhausted from being awake all night listening for her. And the last two nights she's had night sweats. I have to change her pajamas and dry her hair with the hair dryer. It's all just too much."

Hope drained out of me. "Well, I knew things were bad, but she must be getting worse. Well, Bev, at least you know I'm not crazy."

"I just didn't understand how awful it was until I had it right in front of me. Diane, you can't keep doing this alone. Mama will have to spend part of her time down here with me. We've got to take Mama into our homes. No sitter can care for her like we can and you know most nursing homes are hellholes. You know what we went through with Edward's mother. I can't stand for Mama to be in a place like that."

"Well, I don't want her to go into a nursing home. All of them in this area have bad reputations and smell like urine. But when she's up here, she really wants to be in her own house. She seems better when she's there. Don't you think it's important to keep her close to the things she recognizes?"

"I think you're right. Well, when she's there, you'll just have to go back and forth from your house to hers, or keep looking for the right sitter... Oh, Lord. I think I hear her getting up. I'll call you tomorrow. Goodbye!"

I hung up, my stomach in knots. I put on a sweater, went outside and sat in the wooden glider on our back deck. The night air was soft as I swung back and forth and watched a gibbous moon slide in rhythm through the branches of our big old maple trees. My head felt tight with unshed tears. My hound mutt lumbered up and nudged my arm with her muzzle. I let my hand move over her warm back.

Until this call from Bev, I hadn't realized how much I had hoped the dementia was just a bump in the road. Daddy gone, Mama crumbling and now, Bev faltering–it filled me with a sense of doom. I also had to admit how free I felt without the care of Mama since she went to Georgia, but how much I missed her. Even in her strange state, her mere bodily presence was comforting. I remembered how it used to be when Mama and Daddy were still hale and healthy, how I would open the carport door and they would be there, coffee ready, waiting for me to come in and take my place. Those days were gone. Now my sister and I would be the ones making a place for Mama.

I knew Richard and Larkin both loved Mama and wouldn't object to her living with us, but I wondered what lay ahead. Larkin was tiptoeing on the edge of the teen years and sometimes I could feel her unspoken angst moving through the house like a live thing. In her right mind, Mama's presence could provide ballast for those feelings, but I had no idea what her present state would add to the mix. I was glad Richard had his motorcycle obsession to distract him. If things got tense, he could escape to the basement to work on the used Harley he had recently bought.

I bent forward and put my head in my hands. Worry and responsibility dropped down over my shoulders like a sodden overcoat and almost suffocated me. It was not a garment I wanted to wear; but I knew if Mama needed me, I could dress for any occasion. Our relationship was forged not only in love and laughter and family history, not only in the blood kinship of mother and daughter, but twice with the red, sticky stuff of blood itself.

Blood

The scene of the first of our blood connections that I knew of occurred when I was eight and had just had a tonsillectomy. We were living in a small rented house in a rural area of Virginia near Washington, D.C. Daddy was mapping soils in that part of the state.

Many of the details of the scene are blurred, but others stand out with sharp clarity. I remember being ensconced among pillows on the new turquoise blue couch that pulled out into two single beds. We had bought it the week before because Grandma, Mama's mother, was visiting and needed a place to sleep. I was lying there feeling as if I were a contestant on the TV show, "Queen for a Day." I had suffered, and was now reaping benefits.

Grandma and Beverly were busy constructing a dollhouse for me out of a cardboard box, cutting doors and windows and using scraps of colored fabric to fashion curtains and bedspreads for the tiny furniture they were making. Daddy was at work and Mama was in the kitchen stirring up soft custard to ease down my aching throat. The night before I had been allowed to eat as much chocolate ice cream as I wanted and, because sweets were a rarity in our house, I had gorged myself. I recall thinking that that must be the reason I was feeling queasy, and I didn't want to tell anyone for fear all future ice cream rights would be taken away.

But the feeling of nausea grew until I lost interest in the dollhouse and lay with my head back. All at once, I knew it was time to get up and hotfoot it to the bathroom, but before I could rise, I suddenly vomited a large splash of blood into my lap and onto the new couch. In the middle of the bright liquid sat a huge, dark red clot, quivering like cranberry jelly.

The next few moments are not clear. I remember people calling out and a chair turning over, and I can still see Mama's hand picking up the clot and putting it into a glass jar to show the doctor. And I remember her standing at the window, her eyes fixed on the road that would bring the ambulance, every muscle in her body as tense as though they were screaming, "Hurry!"

When things like this happened, Mama never cried or made a fuss. She didn't coddle or cuddle anyone. She put emotions aside and bore her focus down on what needed to be done, her will as forceful and palpable as a locomotive.

The next thing I remember was being rolled out to the waiting ambulance. Because of the cold, someone had covered my head with a sheet and I heard our playmate from next door say, "Is that Diane?" and then, "Is she dead?" I know I must have been in shock, but the romantic poet in me was thinking about what an exciting story this would be to write. Heroic sentences like, "Her head lay in a pool of blood," floated in my mind.

For even more excitement, there was a woman in the ambulance who looked just like a witch. As Mama leaned over me, her eyes fastened to my face, this elderly woman sat impassively on another seat in the back of the rushing vehicle. She wore black, had a thin hooknose and a wart near her chin with two hairs sticking out of it. Even though I was feeling nauseated again, I recall gathering all these details into my memory files for later use. Only one dramatic element was missing—the siren. I was disappointed that there was no rising and falling wail to accompany this rushing journey, which strangely seemed to take place in slow motion.

I vomited again—more blood, bright red, the metallic taste flooding over my tongue, the warmth soaking through my shirt. The witch turned her head and shouted to the driver, "Better hurry. She's hemorrhaging again." Then the siren did come on, but it seemed too loud, too close. The ambulance swayed and rocked. I began to feel weak. The witch seemed to be floating near the ceiling, then outside the windows, big and black in the sky. "Hurry!" her voice whispered close to my ear, "hurry!" Mama knelt beside me and gripped my arms, her ashen face speckled with blood. The fear in her eyes jolted me. Then I realized. This wasn't a story. This was real.

The next thing I recall was being rolled into an emergency room. The nurse flew out from behind the counter to get the doctor. He was a small man with a foreign accent and dark hair who looked not at all surprised to see an eight year-old covered in blood. He asked Mama, coolly, if my operation had been performed in this hospital. She said it had been at St. Jerome's, ten miles away.

"Do you have a doctor here?" he questioned.

"No, but..."

He spoke to the ambulance driver. "Take her on to St. Jerome's," he said and started to turn away.

Mama hurled herself at the doctor. She grabbed his white lapels and jerked his face an inch from hers. A demonic voice came out of her mouth, each word a gunshot. "YOU," she said, "are her doctor and you WILL take her now!"

Later as the doctor bent over me, swabbing my throat, I watched the marks of Mama's bloody hands on his white coat. They looked like tiny dragons, with red plumes of fiery breath. It was only decades later, when I had my own daughter, that I could fully digest the power of that scene. I could understand why Mama never wanted to revisit that urgent winter's day.

When Larkin was in fifth grade I found out about another blood libation that Mama had kept secret from me. Mama, Daddy and I were lingering over coffee one morning and for some reason, we began talking about Rocky Mountain Spotted Fever, a disease caused by tick bite. Daddy said it had once showed up in Mama's blood work because of her transfusion.

I looked over at her in surprise. "What transfusion, Mama? I didn't know you ever had a transfusion."

Mama threw Daddy a look. "Now, Hobart, we don't need to be talking about that!"

But of course, I had to get it out of them, so Daddy told me the story. I knew that Mama and Daddy had been older than most couples when they married and also had had problems conceiving a child. Mama had gotten desperate. Daddy said he thought she'd lose her mind if she couldn't have a baby. They finally found a doctor who could help them, but he warned Mama that her pelvis was narrow and she might have delivery problems. She did. My sister was dragged out with forceps, her head as pointed as a banana when Daddy first saw her. He exclaimed to the nurse, who was a friend of theirs, "My God, Shirley, she's an idiot!" Then he went outside and fainted into the front seat of his car. Shirley sent someone after him and, back in the hospital, showed him how she could rub Bev's head down into a round, perfect baby shape, with no harm done.

Mama was warned not to have any more children, but three years later I was on the way. This time Mama had a cesarean section, which used to be more complicated than it is today. She had an epidural and was awake with no feeling from the waist down. I was born at the University of Virginia teaching hospital in a basement room, which had a low ceiling. The story goes that when the scalpel went into Mama's tight abdomen, water spurted up and hit the ceiling. What Daddy told me for the first time that morning over our cups of coffee was that afterwards Mama began to hemorrhage. They packed her with gauze and she bled through it. They stitched her up and she kept bleeding. Panic set in. Transfusions were given. He didn't know the details, but somehow, she survived.

After Daddy finished the story, Mama got up and headed to the kitchen to refill her coffee cup. "No need to ever go over that again!" The subject was closed.

As I sat on the glider in the moonlight, with Daddy dead and Mama confused, I knew the deep bonds Mama and I had forged in blood and laughter were about to be carried into unknown territory. I thought about the saying, "The only permanent thing we have is change." I knew that change was on the way, had already started. I knew the whiffs of suspicion that Beverly and I had brushed aside with hope and denial had given way to a full-blown, dense, pithy aroma. The elephant was waving its trunk, shuffling its blocky feet, ready to take us for a ride.

"Acquainted with the Night"

If acceptance of the elephant was a big step, the riding of it was another matter. Watching Mama fall victim to this disease seemed to permanently change the color of the sun coming in the window, and yet the light she was continued to shine as brightly as it always had—her love of laughter, her steadfastness, her complex nature that could still surprise us. We wanted more of Mama. We wouldn't give her up.

Because of her love of home, moving Mama out of her house and into ours was a slow transition that took many months. More suitable sitters were hired to help, there were visits to Georgia, and both Sarah and Rachel each spent time staying with Mama in her house. By the time she finally accepted the change, everyone breathed a sigh of relief.

As we settled Mama into the spare bedroom in the upstairs corner of our split-level house, Richard said to me, "Now maybe I'll get to see you once in a while."

None of us realized the changes that living "up close and personal" with Alzheimer's would bring. While in Georgia, a doctor had diagnosed Mama with the disease. There was no turning back.

As my care-giving duties escalated, the thread of this story, which once wound sequentially through my journals, unraveled. Edges blurred together, time was lost. What I recall are scenes endemic to those three years, often out of order, out of focus, reconstructed from memories jarred by haphazard notes in my journals, or on scraps of paper I shoved into a certain drawer.

Overlaying all the memories like a fog was the constant feeling of fatigue. Mama, always a morning person, went to bed sometimes as early as eight and I, the night owl, latched onto that free time to spend with my family or my own pursuits. It helped keep me sane, even though I knew that later she would probably be up and on the prowl.

Mama roamed the night for a variety of reasons, and I learned to sleep with "one ear open." The sound of her knocks on our bedroom door became the dreaded knell of sleep deprivation. No matter how confused, she was always able to find our room, which was across the hall and one down from hers. Some nights Mama used the bathroom but couldn't find her way back into her room, and other nights she thought it was time to get up every few hours throughout the night. She would knock again and again, asking anxiously about breakfast, and her whereabouts. Often the only way to calm her was to go back into her room and squeeze onto the single bed against her small, bony form.

Other times she had night sweats. After she rapped on our door I would stumble out into the hall, and she would be feeling her collar with both hands, her eyes wide and round.

"I'm wringing wet!" she would exclaim as though it were a new and dangerous development. Back in her bedroom, I changed her pajama top and used the hairdryer, fluffing up her fine, short hair with one hand. Then she usually asked to be sprinkled with floral powder. By the time we completed this ritual, I was wide-awake, but Mama dropped into sleep the minute her dry head hit the pillow.

Sometimes I went back to my bed and lay there staring at the ceiling, fighting the night fiends of worry and despair until I fell into the slumber of exhaustion. Other times I would scoot over and spoon Richard's back, inhaling his scent and warming myself with his body heat until these physical comforts lulled me into sleep.

My sister and I spent many phone hours trying to find a potion to keep Mama in bed at night. An enthusiast of natural remedies, I tried to calm Mama's nighttime roaming with the herbal remedies of valerian, hops, skullcap, melatonin and sometimes, sherry. I soothed her with lavender sachets and castor oil packs. I ran a humidifier in the winter and a fan in summer, hoping the noise would ease her into an unbroken sleep.

When these failed, my sister called in the doctors and they prescribed sleeping pills, anti-hallucinogenics, anti-epilepsy drugs and nerve medicine. But the side effects were sometimes worse than the benefits. Mama experienced incontinence, dizziness and lethargy. She had a hard time swallowing pills, and liquor drove her blood pressure up.

We tried daytime naps, together on my bed, but I would just be tumbling into the lovely embrace of REM when Mama would sit up and want to know if it was time to get up and when we were going to go "home."

Bev's and my search for rest was never satisfied, and we learned to do with bits and pieces of slumber until Mama went to the other sister, after which I once slept for twelve straight hours. One particular night stands out in my memory because after that nighttime encounter, sleep did not return the rest of the night. It was the first time I had to admit that Mama no longer recognized me as her daughter.

It was 4:20 a.m. when Mama rapped again on our bedroom door. It was the fifth time that night. The raps were loud and sharp, so I knew her anxiety was up, despite the pills I had given her earlier. Richard groaned and rolled over. I dragged myself to the door and saw Mama standing in the dim light of the hall with her suitcase. She had put on two pairs of flowered pink pajama tops with her bra fastened over them. She sported brown wool pants with her black snow boots on the wrong feet, so that her toes stuck out at ridiculous angles. On her head was her tan, broad-brimmed traveling hat. If it hadn't been so sad, I'd have laughed.

"I want to go home," she announced in a troubled voice. Her eyes darted fearfully around the hall.

"Mama, you are home. You live here now with me and Richard and Larkin." I stroked her arm. "See your room and your cozy bed?"

She jerked her arm away and grimaced at me. "Stop trying to fool me. I've got to get home. My mama is waiting for me. She doesn't know where I am. She'll be worried. She's waiting for me." Her brow furrowed and her lower lip trembled.

I turned on the overhead light so she could see me. "Mama, you can't go home just now. You..."

She clomped toward the stairs. "I AM going now. I want to go HOME."

I caught her before she started down. "OK, you can go, but let's get your clothes on right. You don't want to go home without your sweater and coat. Your clothes are a little mixed up. And don't you want to go to the bathroom before you go?" I hoped to break this traveling trend.

She stared at me suspiciously, and then relented. "OK, I'll go to the bathroom." I left her alone for a minute, and then returned.

"It's all right," I announced in a bright voice, "I've called your mother, and she wants you to wait until daylight to come home. Let's just lie down till then."

She came out the bathroom door. "She isn't worried?" Her fingers plucked at her pajama sleeves.

"No, I told her you are coming at daylight. Let's lie down."

"She knows I'm coming?"

"Yes, she does."

"She knows I'm coming." Mama repeated. A moment of relief played across her face.

"Come on," I urged. "We'll rest until then."

She leaned heavily on my arm on the way back to bed. We fixed her clothes.

"Do you want me to lie down with you for a while?" I asked.

"Yes, please." Her voice was like a tired child's.

We lay there, scrunched side by side. All my cells sagged with weariness, but I couldn't sleep. I watched her profile: the high forehead, the strongly molded nose. I thought of the many times I had studied its strength, and I realized how much it comforted me, even at this strange time in our lives.

Suddenly she turned to me. "Do you have a mother?" she whispered confidentially.

"Yes, I have a mother," I finally whispered back.

"Where is she?"

For a moment I could not speak. Grief lay like a small stone against my lips. Then I took a breath and answered. "My mother is waiting for me, too. Somewhere, she's waiting for me."

Trading Mama

Bev and I traded Mama back and forth every month to six weeks, depending on what was happening in our lives. Sometimes we combined this with a visit, but often we met at the Huntersville exit, number 27 off Interstate 77. This exit was about halfway between our homes and far enough outside Charlotte, North Carolina, to be free of traffic congestion. We met at Wendy's. Since Mama hardly ever ate away from home, even fast food was a treat. She loved the salty French fries and always wanted to get at least two of the small white paper ketchup cups for dipping.

I remember this particular trading time because I began to notice the relationship of two things: Mama's memory loss and my weight. Bev and I both gained pounds having Mama in our homes. I figured it was because she wanted three square meals a day and we enjoyed them right along with her. That, plus her penchant for ice cream, which we both ate often. But the emotional component of my eating became very evident on this particular trip.

"Where is it we're going?" Mama asked, craning her neck at the Technicolor spring season that was streaming past the car windows as we zoomed south down I-81. We were in her old gray Chevy Caprice Classic that we all referred to as "the boat" because of its roominess and the way it wallowed down the highway. Mama was looking good in the new blue cotton sweater I'd bought her. We had put on her makeup and she was sporting her new white traveling visor. You'd never have known from the vividness of her eyes that she had been up six times the previous night, knocking on my door with a variety of questions, mostly about where her bed was and when we were going to go "home."

I, on the other hand, awoke puffed and blotchy and dressed myself in the same drab blue sweat suit I'd worn the day before. It seemed to be the only thing that fit me after our weeks of eating at least two bowls of ice cream a day and getting little exercise, not to mention sleep.

I gripped the steering wheel and tried to blink the grit out of my eyes. Be in the moment, I told myself. Be Carlos Castaneda, lose your personal history. Pretend she hadn't asked that question at least one hundred times already on the first hour of this three-hour trip.

I forced cheerfulness into my voice. "We're going to Huntersville, North Carolina, Mama, to meet Beverly. You know, we'll meet her at the Wendy's there. You love to go to Wendy's. You love the French fries."

"Beverly?"

"Yes," I replied heartily. "She's your oldest daughter. The one with dark brown hair."

"Oh yes, the pretty one!"

Whoa! This was not the answer I expected. Never had Mama said one of us was prettier or smarter than the other. She praised us for our accomplishments and sometimes looks, but never compared. One time Bev had asked her, as children do, which one she loved the best and she had answered, "Whoever is the sickest."

I'm sure her answer was because we had both suffered difficult-to-diagnose childhood illnesses and Mama had spent so much time worrying over us. I'm sure she meant she was more focused on the one who was most ill, but I often wonder now when a sickness is my bid for love and attention.

Though I knew that Mama didn't know who I was at that moment, I was surprised that the comment hurt my feelings. I have never thought that my looks were my strong suit, but I also didn't think my sister was *that* much better looking, although she did have an air about her that Mama called "to the manor born." Beverly had an aura of poise and gentility and seemed to know how to dress and what to do in social situations. I was more of the ilk of "to the cave born," more comfortable in the woods or fishing in the river. I always seemed to have a string hanging loose or mismatched socks.

I sighed. "I'm your younger daughter, Mama. You just have us two girls."

Mama stared out through the windshield in deep thought. "Well, if I have children, I must have a husband."

"Well, you did have a husband. Hobart Porter. He died three years ago. But you had fifty-four wonderful years together."

"Fifty-four years!" As usual, she was incredulous at this.

Then she dropped her voice and leaned toward me, "Did we get along?"

"Very well, for being married that long. No marriage is perfect, but you were lucky. You complemented each other. He used to hunt and you would cook the game—quail and deer and turkey. And fish...you loved to cook up those bass and redeye."

"Well!" This seemed to satisfy her greatly.

Then after a moment of deep thought, "Did we ever have any children?"

Oh, God, here it comes. The same old round robin of questions I had listened to until I was dotty.

"Yes, Beverly and I are your two girls." To distract her, I segued into a rapid, descriptive monologue. "Look,

Mama, at that fruit tree blooming all by itself in the middle of that field! Isn't that a beautiful spring sight? And look at that old tumbledown barn. You know, Mama, now that the big corporations are taking over the farming industry, the small, family-owned farms will soon be a thing of the past; so you won't see many old barns like that." Mama was paying no attention to my chatter. "We better enjoy them while we can. Let's keep our eyes peeled for the next old barn. I think there's one just over this hill and look at the green. I love the early spring green. There's the barn!"

I babbled at top speed. "You know the only good thing about the farming situation is that a lot of the smaller farms are going organic, and I've noticed that even though organic food doesn't have preservatives, it stays fresh much longer than the food with all those preservatives in it that you can't even pronounce. One of my friends says if you can't pronounce it, you shouldn't eat it. Haha, I think that's a good rule to live by, or should I say eat by..."

Mama was leaning toward me, gripping her knees with both hands and peering at me intently. Finally she said in a troubled voice, "Are you kin to me?"

"Yes." My voice deflated. "Yes, I'm your daughter, Diane. *The homely one.*"

"Oh, right." She settled happily back in her seat, then pulled up her collar with one hand and craned her neck into the back seat. "There's not a window open, is there? I feel a draft."

"No, I know you can't stand any air blowing on you."

Chronically cold natured, Mama couldn't abide open windows and we didn't even mention air conditioning unless it was a hundred degrees outside. Neither could

she stand any sort of radio—music, talk show or news—
that might distract us as we traveled.

She gazed out the side window. "Are we going
somewhere or are we just out for a drive?"

"Just a springtime drive," I murmured dully. Then my
hand reached out of its own accord and took a chocolate
kiss from the bag on the console. I held the steering wheel
with my elbow while I unwrapped the kiss and popped it
into my mouth. The flood of sugar and chocolate was
heavenly. The thick smear of it against the insides of my
mouth as I moved it around with my tongue was divine.
Even though I had told myself the bag of kisses was for
Mama, I now told myself I would have as many as I
wanted, and maybe even stop and buy a new bag for the
return trip.

"There certainly are a lot of dead cats along this road."
Mama's tone was slightly indignant.

"What?"

"Dead cats, and some must be kittens, they're so
small. I wonder what's killing them." Mama shook her
head.

"What, Mama, what are you talking about?" I
scrutinized the sides of the road.

"Dead cats. They're all along this road. It's sad, even
though you know I don't like cats."

I grabbed another candy and pushed it into my
mouth, stopping the urge to laugh and scream at the
same time. *Was Mama starting to hallucinate?* "Where
are they, Mama? Show me one."

"There! Right there on the side of the road!" Mama
was pointing to a black piece of tire that had shredded off
of an eighteen-wheeler. I scanned it as we passed and had
to admit that I could conjure up the carcass of a cat out of
the twisted rubber.

I handed her the bag of candy. "Have a kiss." Maybe watching for dead cats and eating chocolate would keep the question loop from starting up again. I hunched over the wheel, staring at the white lines.

We were almost to Huntersville. The return trip loomed like a carrot at the end of a stick. First, I would stop and buy a new bag of kisses, perhaps the kind that contains almonds. And because it would be hot by that time of day, I'd have as much air conditioning as I wanted and I'd play as much music as I wanted, as loud as I desired. I smiled to myself as I remembered the last time I got Mama back from Bev. Two days later my sister had called me. "Guess what I'm doing?" she had asked in a cocky tone.

"What?"

"Riding around with the windows open and the radio on—full blast!" We had both chortled.

As I pulled onto the exit ramp, Mama asked, "Where are we?"

"Huntersville, Mama. We're going to stop and eat something. "

"Oh, good." She felt for her visor and straightened it.

I scanned the parking lot for Bev's gold Camry. There it was. She was already there. Relief washed through me as I thought of sleeping through a whole night with no interruptions. But when I glanced at Mama I felt a pang. I would miss her presence in my life for the next six weeks. When it was time to trade her back, I knew we'd have a "honeymoon phase," when just having her with me would make everything seem better. This would last perhaps a week, until lack of sleep began to tell on me again.

"Here we are, Mama. Wendy's!"

Bev looked great. She wore a new red L.L. Bean shirt and khakis. Her hair was glossy and she had on makeup.

The one who was receiving Mama always looked good, well groomed and rested. The one passing her off was usually bleary eyed and unkempt.

Mama stared at Bev for a moment, and then relaxed as she realized it was someone she knew. "Oh, it's you!" We all hugged and then ordered food. Mama always had a hamburger and French fries and a small Frosty for dessert.

As we ate we tried to clue Mama in on where she'd be going and who would be there. At one point she realized that I wouldn't be going with her.

Her face fell. "You're leaving me, then?"

She was like a sad child until I assured her that she'd soon be coming back to be with me. It was like old times sitting there eating and chatting about the family. For a moment I pretended that Daddy was not dead, but somewhere roaming the woods with his buddies during spring gobbler season while Mama, in her right mind, was having an outing with us girls.

But the moment passed and it was time to go. I held Mama to me for a long minute, enjoying her powdery smell. Her bones felt as fragile as those of a baby animal. I left first and looked back to wave goodbye. Mama and Beverly were still sitting there in a rosy glow from the sun coming in the window. Bev waved and Mama smiled and raised her tiny white ketchup cup to me in a farewell salute, then delicately took a sip from it as though tasting the finest of wines.

I laughed and cried and popped Hershey's kisses in my mouth all the way home, with the music blaring and the air conditioner turned up high.

Men

In the mornings after breakfast, Mama and I often danced to "Boot Scootin' Boogie" by Brooks and Dunn. I would fix her usual meal of coffee, one soft-boiled egg on toast and sausage or crisp bacon. We ate this hearty meal together in the kitchen on the round bistro table after Richard and Larkin had eaten their cold cereal and left for work and school.

Often Mama cleaned her plate by throwing bits of food to our two dogs, both red-colored mutts, who began expectantly flanking our breakfast every morning. Sipsy, half basset and half redbone coonhound, looked like a cartoon dog with her trailing ears, short legs and straight up tail. She would prance in place, almost snapping Mama's fingers off while gobbling bits of toast and bacon. Floyd, a golden retriever mix who had lost one eye to a cat, sat calmly in his scalloped curls, taking the food so slowly and delicately from Mama's hands that Sipsy sometimes snaked out her head and sucked the food right off his lips. Floyd would give Sipsy a long, disappointed, one-eyed stare and edge a bit closer to the table. Although I had asked Mama not to feed the dogs at mealtimes, of course she forgot and relished the doggy drama so much that I soon looked forward to it as much as she did. She always referred to both dogs as "he."

After breakfast I would ask, "Do you want to dance this morning, Mama?"

"Of, course!" was her most frequent answer.

We moved into the living room. I pressed number four on the CD player, where "Boot Scootin' Boogie" stayed keyed up ready to play.

The country rhythm set our feet moving as the deep male voices rolled around us. Mama spun with a ladylike flare. She moved in wide circles, patting out one foot, then the other as she turned, gracefully swiping at the air with open hands. Every now and then she cut her eyes over at me, raised her eyebrows and smiled as if to say, "Is this not the best fun ever?"

I moved as fast as I could, trying to cram a full-fledged workout into one song's time, all the while savoring the taste of bacon on the back of my tongue. The dogs sat together on the sidelines, an attentive audience of two.

After a couple of verses, Mama was ready to sit on the couch and study the CD cover where Brooks and Dunn look out with overt cowboy raunch. She stared at the photo of the two men, one with his hip cocked out behind his guitar, the other with a knowing grin as wide as his Stetson.

"Nice looking men!" she exclaimed. She never wanted to dance to female singers. There was something about those low-slung manly voices that activated her. I guess you're never too old. In fact, the whole family noticed that Mama, in her late eighties and with Alzheimer's, had gotten a little boy-crazy.

Maybe it was because she didn't remember she'd ever been married, plus not knowing her age. Before her dementia, Mama had told me she was often startled to look in the mirror, because in her heart, she was still sixteen. According to today's psychology, her affinity for men could be tied to a longing for the intimate male figure that her enigmatic father had never been. Or the reason could simply be that Mama, like many women, had always been highly interested in romance.

When we were teenagers, she had devised a guessing game for us in order to hone our instincts in choosing a mate. We usually played the game as we three women were lounging on Mama's bed, our favorite retreat for talking about the world and our place in it. Mama's questions were always fairly transparent, and we rarely failed to choose the correct answer.

"Beverly," Mama, propped up on three pillows, would begin, "You have a beau who has inherited plenty of money and already owns that big farm you've always dreamed of. He's tall and handsome and he knows it, so he flirts with other women. He also drinks too much but has sworn to you that he will quit both habits once you're married."

She modulated her voice so we wouldn't get any clues as to the right answer. "Your other beau is tall but not as good-looking, although he has laughing eyes and a kind smile. This man is not well-to-do but has a good job and knows how to save his money. He isn't a flirt and doesn't drink. He doesn't know much about farming, but is interested in hearing you talk about it. You are equally attracted to both men. Whom would you choose?" Bev and I would exchange glances, and she would pretend to study the question before she chose the latter. Then it would be my turn.

Although most of the questions were no-brainers, the games must have served us well, as my sister and I have remained married for decades to our original mates.

The first time I realized Mama was still interested in romance for herself was after Daddy was gone and her dementia had already set in; the time she made a fool of herself over Mason.

Mason and Daddy were good hunting buddies and had taught together at the university. He was a thin, wiry man, with a shy, reserved manner; was unmarried and devoted his attentions to his ailing mother who lived in his home. Every Christmas, he would bring Mama and Daddy a poinsettia. He continued to bring Mama poinsettias after Daddy died and I believe Mama got it in her head that he was courting her.

The second Christmas after Daddy was gone, I was with Mama at her house when Mason called and asked if he could come by. After I prepped her on the salient facts about him, Mama seemed to remember who he was. Just before time for him to arrive, she went into the bedroom and put on her best red sweater and a touch of makeup. Mama was still an attractive woman for her age and I wondered if Mason had ever noticed her as anything but his friend's wife.

When he arrived, carrying a large pink variety of the holiday flower, Mama greeted him and exclaimed over the poinsettia like it was the prettiest thing she had ever seen. She placed it in the middle of the coffee table, poured Mason a cup of coffee, and soon they were chatting and catching up on the past year. I excused myself to pay some bills, but sat at the dining room table where I could watch Mama being her most charming self, praising the elderly man for taking such good care of his mother. I found myself mesmerized as she began to do some outright flirting, talking about what a strong-looking man he was.

A quizzical look came over Mason's face, and then he slowly began to redden as the tenor of her mood dawned on him. He got the message fully when Mama patted the sofa next to her and said, smoothing her skirt with her other hand, "Why don't you come over here and sit by me, Mason?"

Instead Mason jumped to his feet and said in a loud voice, "Ah, no! I...I've got to go take the other poinsettias to people. I, ah, have a lot of them in the car. I have a list of people I take them to, you know." He was trying to let Mama know she wasn't any more special that anyone else on his list, but she didn't take the hint.

"You have to go already? Won't you stay for one more cup of coffee?" she said with a coquettish air.

When he demurred, she followed him as he almost ran out the front door. She posed in the open doorway and sent out her best Southern cliché, "Well, you come back and see me real soon, you hear."

She stood there, waving as he drove away. "Well, I hope HE comes back to visit," she mused to herself.

Inside my chest, bemusement tussled with irritation. Was I upset that Daddy's place in her heart was so easily usurped, even with this dread disease? Or was I embarrassed that my elderly mother had gone boy-crazy?

"Mama, it's time for a little ice cream." My voice was sharp.

Her interest in romance continued with family members. Once Bev and her husband, Edward, took Mama with them on a drive to peruse a neighborhood of super upscale new homes. Mama rode quietly in the back seat and when they returned home and settled in, Bev asked, "Did you enjoy the ride, Mama?"

"Oh, yes." Mama replied, "and..." She motioned Bev to come closer and dropped her voice, "You know that man that was riding in the front seat? Well, I think he's interested in you."

My niece, Sarah, and I noticed Mama's interest in men one night when we were preparing dinner. Sarah had moved into Mama's house to attend graduate school in Animal Science, and her assistance with Mama was priceless. After a grueling day in the barn, she often came over to help me cook. To diffuse stress she and I had concocted a colorful cast of characters, all probably politically incorrect, that we mimicked while cooking. There were the "Barrio Boys," who loved spicy food, the "Valley Girls", who were catty, and Forrest Gump's cousin, Camilla, who had a low IQ, but high emotional intelligence. One evening when we were immersed in being the "Barrio Boys," complete with low voices and accents, we noticed Mama kept coming into the kitchen and looking around with a confused air. Finally she asked, "Did I hear some men in here? Are they coming to dinner?"

Richard caught the full brunt of Mama's attentions one evening when he took care of Mama while I attended a meeting. When I turned my cell phone back on, there was a series of calls from him.

"Diane, can you give me a call, soon?"

"Diane, can you please call me as soon as you're done?"

"Ah, Diane, I need you to call me right away!"

"Diane, where ARE you?"

Richard had taken Mama out for a drive and she got it into her mind that they were on a date. When they returned to our house, he said Diane should be home soon and Mama asked who Diane was. When he answered that Diane was his wife, Mama went berserk. "Your wife?" she screamed. "You have a wife? Why, you two-timer! All this time with me, and you have a wife?" She brandished her cane and then hurled it at Richard, striking him in the knees. "Take me home this minute! Where is the car? Take me home!" She marched to the door and flung it open. Richard hobbled after, calling me on his cell phone before he drove over to Mama's old home while Mama sat in stony silence.

"This is not my house!" Mama shrieked from the car. "I said, 'take me home!'"

Usually, when Mama insisted on going "home," we drove her about, stopping at a store, chatting about other things, until she forgot the purpose of the drive. But this evening, fueled by two-timing, she glowered and fumed and demanded while Richard drove round and round, calling me as surreptitiously as he could manage, lest Mama think he was calling yet another girlfriend. He and I arrived at our house at the same moment, and I have seldom seen him so glad to see me.

Delicate Bathroom Tricks

In my thirties I wrote a poem containing only one good line—"delicate bathroom tricks." It concerned a father taking his daughter to the restroom during a church service. Although the poem ended up in my trashcan, the phrase often flashed into my mind as I cleaned up the bathroom after Mama.

In her right mind, Mama was such a refined and fastidious person about bathroom matters, that I am wary of writing about this topic. She considered bodily functions normal, but not part of everyday discourse. The correct anatomical words for body parts were also not part of her repertoire. When I was five years old, while taking a bath with a younger boy cousin, I pointed to his privates and asked Mama, "What's that?" After a moment's silence, I was told it was a "butterball," forever tainting my appetite at Thanksgiving dinners where Butterball Turkeys are served.

The closest thing to an off-color joke I ever heard Mama repeat was a story from her childhood that was passed down in the family annals from her mother's large family of ten siblings, back in the days of outhouses and chamber pots.

In the story, after a party at my grandmother's house, one young suitor was still dawdling about downstairs with the youngest daughter, Bea. The five other sisters had gone upstairs to bed.

"Bea, has Bob gone home yet?" her sister Fanny called down.

Bob, thinking they might say something nice about him, whispered to Bea, "Tell 'em yes. Tell 'em yes."

"Yes." Bea's voice floated up.

"Well," hollered Fanny, "you better piss before you come up. The pot's running over!"

It is said that Bob faded into the night without a word.

Mama also told us the story of her extended stay in the family outhouse. When she was a teen, she was in the facility one hot summer day when a family from their church arrived unexpectedly on a Sunday afternoon visit. The youngest member of the family happened to be a boy in her school class. Her mother settled the visitors in the grove, with the outhouse barely in view down a winding path, and served lemonade. Not knowing where her daughter was, Grandma kept calling Mama to come and visit with the guests. But rather than be seen coming out of such an embarrassing place, Mama stayed in the stifling enclosure for several hours until the visitors left. When they departed, she stumbled forth, rushed to drink the dregs of the lemonade and then collapsed into the shade of the densest tree and lay there an hour to recover.

I was grateful that Mama wasn't cognizant enough to be embarrassed about using Depends by the time she needed them, which was about three years into her dementia. After she used them for a year, a friend mentioned to me that Mama's Alzheimer's medicine could cause incontinence, of both bowel and bladder. Since the medicine didn't seem to be helping the dementia, we stopped it, and within a month, she was out of diapers. I was glad, for both of us, to give her bathroom privacy back to Mama.

But during that year there were stories to be gathered. Such as the morning when I was taking Mama to the bathroom clad only in her Depends and an undershirt.

Suddenly a ball of poop popped out of the side of her diaper and rolled in slow motion down the hall. Our hound, Sipsy, ever alert to chase anything small and moving, took off after it and the dog and I had a race for the darn thing. Just at the top of the stairs, Sipsy won, and bolted it down like a chocolate.

"What in the world was that?" Mama asked, peering around the bathroom door.

I always said I didn't really mind the Depends year that much, but stress has a way of manifesting, as happened one evening. After getting Mama settled for the night, I often tried to go out with my dogs for a walk. Just entering the fields near our house, smelling the earth, looking at the stars, listening for the owls that called back and forth, was medicine for my spirit. It made me feel as though I had, if not a life of my own, at least "a field of my own."

One night I went out when I should have gone to bed. I trudged through a light snow, feeling stupid with exhaustion. As I looked up at the high end of the field where my two dogs moved in dark shapes against the white expanse, all I could do was wonder why those two pieces of poop were moving on their own, and how I was going to get them into the toilet. When I came to my senses, I vowed to choose bed over field more often.

Many other "bathroom stories" were garnered from those years. There was the time I walked in to find Mama brushing her teeth with Preparation H, and the morning she emerged from the bathroom wearing my daughter's underpants on her head like a cap. Another time, after she had vacated the premises, I went in to find the large industrial size plunger from the back of the closet sitting upright in the middle of the bathroom floor, with an unused roll of toilet paper stuck down over the handle. I gave up ever figuring out that scenario.

The saddest incident occurred one evening when Mama called me into the bathroom. She stood there in front of the toilet, pants around her ankles, and held out a handful of excrement. She shook her head a bit and said, "I don't know what this is, but it came from right back here," and she delicately patted her bottom with her other hand.

And I was totally flummoxed one winter morning when Mama had been in the bathroom with the water running for about fifteen minutes. Worried, I stood outside the door and asked her what she was doing in there.

"Oh, just washin' my pussy." She replied casually. I nearly choked. Didn't even know she knew the word.

Some evenings, after she had been in bed for hours, I would look up the stairs and see Mama emerge from the bathroom. With her eyes round and her hair standing on end, she looked like a small denizen of the night, a creature out of Sendak's, *Where the Wild Things Are.* Often she stared at me, probably wondering who I was, and then hightailed it back to her room and closed the door. If she didn't seem upset, I just let her go, grateful for a few hours of peace.

But on occasion my tired brain entertained strange thoughts. Sometimes I found myself thinking that maybe night is her time to transform. By day she was an elderly lady with dementia, by night she became another being who performed "delicate bathroom tricks" to amuse herself and confound others. As it was, I always opened the door to the bathroom warily, never able to anticipate what I might find.

Peace

Move over and make room, Ram Das, Pema Chödrön, Eckhart Tolle. Mama has become my foremost teacher of a skill I have been trying to learn from your books for years–how to live in the present moment.

It was the third autumn of Mama's dementia. She and I were sitting side by side on my tan living room couch, looking across the room out of the large window that spans half the wall. The leaves that flamed into brilliant color against crystal blue heavens now lay in sodden heaps under a sky as gray and fuzzy as the fur of my cat that was stretched out on the wide windowsill.

Though I was sitting quite still, tears still stung my eyelids and my mind whirled like a carousel that I couldn't stop, the same old thoughts coming around again and again: *I can't believe I said what I said. What will I do next? Could I ever hurt Mama? Winter is coming. I'll be trapped. I'm so tired. I can't do this anymore...*

It had been a bad morning. Even though Mama had only waked me twice during the night, I had overslept and Larkin missed the bus. Richard was out of town, so I bundled Mama into the car with us to race my daughter to school. When we pulled up, another "soccer mom" was on her way into the building, probably to assist in art class, something I used to do before Mama moved in with us. The woman waved and called, "see you at the game." and my heart sank. I realized I had forgotten that it was our turn to provide the half time snack for Larkin's team for a game that was an hour's drive away.

The problem was that Mama had dropped her dentures and cracked them the day before, and I had arranged an emergency date with the dentist for four o'clock, just the time I should be driving toward the soccer field. It was Friday, so Mama wouldn't have teeth for the weekend if I didn't keep the appointment. Not a terrible thing except I would have to fix special foods and one of her old friends was coming to visit on Sunday. I didn't want Mama to be toothless.

Gathering her books, Larkin saw my look of concern. "You didn't forget soccer, did you? You know we have snack. Dad's not even going to be there!"

"Of course not." I lied, as she slammed out of the car.

You can do this, I told myself as I pulled away. *It's just a scheduling problem.*

But frustration began gnawing at my midsection. This would be easy if Richard were home. Last year he never missed a game. And it wasn't like he was away on business. More and more frequently he left to go to yet another motorcycle rally. At first he attended the ones close by. Then he went farther and farther afield, roaring off on his turquoise-and-white Harley, clad elegantly in black leather, while I stood in my sweats at the window, Mama in tow.

I thought of my sister, who said that when Mama was with her, her husband had begun disappearing earlier and earlier into his den after work, carrying his martini and closing the door tightly behind him. Once, after she left Mama with him for an hour, he was already sequestered in the den when she came home. Mama met Bev at the door and said, as though bearing important news, "There's a preacher in the house. He's in that room."

Though she didn't ask, Bev wondered if Mama had mistaken him for a preacher because the Lord's name had been invoked in some form. The last time we had talked, Bev said of our husbands, "They've done awfully well, but they're wearing down." I knew she was referring to all of us.

I wheeled the car up to the McDonald's window, thinking maybe a treat would help get us through the day, before I remembered Mama's lack of teeth. So I got myself an egg Mc Muffin, with two coffees.

"Don't open this until we get home." I stuck Mama's cup behind me in the backseat holder where Mama was sitting. But we hadn't gone two blocks before Mama screamed, "Ow, ow, ouch." I pulled to the curb, jumped out and jerked open the back door. Mama was holding her leg, coffee all over the floor. Luckily it wasn't a bad burn, thanks to her long pants and rain boots. I calmed Mama down and as I got back in the front seat, blue flashing lights pulled up behind us. I got out and explained the situation to the lanky policeman who swaggered up. He peered at Mama, saw the coffee, and then barked, "This is not a stopping area. Get going!" He slapped his hand on the car. The gnawing worsened.

At home, we changed Mama's clothes, spread on some first aid cream and got her ensconced at the kitchen table while I stirred up some Cream of Wheat, my egg McMuffin lying forgotten in the car. *I guess I can call around to see if anyone else can trade snack times with me. Larkin will be upset. Or maybe I should just go on and take Mama to the dentist early. While I'm in the waiting room, maybe I can take a little nap. I'm so tired. I don't think I can't do this anymore...*

Mama's voice cut through my thoughts. "Are you kin to me?"

As she started the same old cycle of questions, the gnawing in my solar plexus crawled into my chest, into my head. My temples throbbed. When she got to the question, "Well, did I have a husband?" I turned and glared at her. She sat there holding her cup of coffee with both hands, looking at me expectantly. In my mind's eye, I saw myself stride across the kitchen with a roar and smash the cup out of her hands to the floor. Instead I turned away, gripped the edge of the stove and said in a calm voice, "No, you were never married. No one ever wanted you. Or me either. We're both old maids—spinsters, living here alone."

There was a long silence in which, strangely enough, I began to feel relief from the throbbing. I felt lighter. I stirred the Cream of Wheat blurringly fast. *Maybe I should say something else. Something really bad, like we had been in jail...*

A soft hand touched my shoulder. I turned and Mama stood there with a sorrowful expression on her face. Her eyes were moist. "I am so sorry," she said, shaking her head. "You're such a sweet person. I can't understand why no one would want you."

"Excuse me," I said. I brushed past Mama, went into the bathroom and closed the door. I leaned against the wall and cried. I cried because my own mother no longer knew me. I cried because I was acting like a mean child. I cried for everything we had both lost. Then I remembered that Mama was standing by the stove where a hot pot of cereal was cooking, and I bolted back to the kitchen, wiped my eyes, and dished up the food.

I led her and her cereal bowl to the couch, where I explained that I was just kidding, just making a joke. Eating silently, she ignored me, and I'm not sure she even remembered. We sat. Tears were still prickling my eyes, but the gnawing was gone, and I was left with a hollow feeling, a feeling that something had been broken.

But the mind didn't stop. The mind was relentless. *I can't believe I said what I said. What will I do next? Winter is coming. I'll be trapped. I'm so tired. I can't do this anymore.*

Mama set her bowl on the coffee table. "I'm getting chilly."

"I'll get your sweater." I went upstairs, my mind getting louder with every step. *I can't believe I said what I said. What will I do next? Winter is coming...*

I took her sweater from the closet and as I turned to the door, the sweater caught on a book that was poking out of the bookcase. A slender paperback fell to the floor and I bent to retrieve it. *Peace Is Every Step: The Path of Mindfulness in Everyday Life,* by Tich Nat Hanh. It seemed like something from another life, something I would never have a chance to read. My mind kept up its rhythm. *I can't believe I said what I said. What will I do next? Winter...* I placed the book back on the shelf, and then stood perfectly still. Deep within me, realization resounded like a loud gong.

"Everyday life," I whispered. "Peace."

Everything I'd ever read about being in the present moment streamed over my body in a rush.

Stop! Just stop! I screamed to my mind. And another phrase from a long ago book floated up, "To find the present moment, you have to lose your mind and come to your senses."

Mama's sweater was very soft against my arm. The bordered weave of color, pink and blue against a darker blue, formed just the right contrast. I started down the stairs, the heels of my shoes heavier than the toes, the sound clunky, the banister under my hand cool and smooth to the touch. Mama sat hunched over on the couch, her hair, still much brown among the gray, feathered softly around her ears. She turned her face to me, her blue eyes bright as azure in her soft wrinkles. I felt her bony shoulders as I slipped the sweater around her. Her breath, when she thanked me, smelled of brown sugar and milk. I sat close and took her hand. It was as dry and thin as one of the leaves that drifted past the window. The cat, still reclining on the sill, meowed and lifted her head to look at us. Her fur was backlit into a silver areole around the gray. The smell of coffee lingered in the air.

Beside me, Mama's body was warm. Her hand heated up in mine. I turned to her and she smiled happily. Even though she was without teeth, it was a smile I had known all my life. I looked at her little body and thought, *this is the body that helped form the helix of my DNA.* And I began to laugh, because it had taken such a short time for my mind to think such different thoughts.

"What's funny?" Mama asked.

"Everything," I replied, and that satisfied her. She squeezed my hand.

We sat and our breath took on the same rhythm. In and out, in and out. I was sitting with my mother on a fall day, in my home. We were together and we were warm and we were watching my cat in the window with occasional leaves floating by. We were alive. We breathed. Again tears came to my eyes, but instead of tears of frustration or despair, the tears flowed from the feeling that was drenching me, drenching Mama, the room, the window, the cat—the exquisite sweetness of that one moment in time, that present moment.

Coming Apart

As great as the gift of the present moment continued to be, I learned that to be present in some moments is much easier than being present in others. Hovering over Mama's supine form in an emergency room cubicle for an interminable wait, while through the crack of the curtains I could see hospital personnel drinking cokes and laughing, was not a good moment. But this moment began to repeat itself when Mama started having what Bev and I called "spells," for lack of any medical term. The only thing any doctor told us, late in the game, was that they were perhaps caused by interactions of some of her medicines.

The first time it happened was at Bev's home. Mama knocked on her bedroom door in the night, and when Bev came out, Mama was on the floor, unconscious. By the time the paramedics arrived, Mama had awakened, and they made a chair of their hands to carry her down the stairs to the waiting ambulance. A thorough checkout in the hospital revealed nothing.

After rushing to the hospital numerous times and consulting with her doctors, Bev and I became watchful but blasé about the "spells." After she rested for a short while, Mama always rallied and seemed none the worse for the experience. We knew that she would be better off reviving at home, rather than waiting in a chilly emergency room and going through another set of tests that would tell us nothing.

Her last "spell" that I recall occurred one spring afternoon after she and I attended Larkin's local soccer game, and it probably established me, in some people's minds, as someone capable of elder abuse.

After a thrilling game, Larkin's team won, and we waved her off to go celebrate with a group of teammates. Mama took my arm, and we were near the car when she suddenly stumbled and sagged against me. When I realized she was unconscious, I called for help and several other soccer parents came running. We got Mama into the front seat. I tossed my purse in back and, by reflex, clicked the lock switch before closing the door. Mama, eyes closed and mouth open, head lolling back against the seat, was locked in. The key, of course, was in my purse. The other parents crowded around, excitedly offering to call a locksmith, get a coat hanger, break the window. They stared at me in surprise when I dismissed their ideas and leaned against the car to wait. "It's really O.K. This happens all the time," I tried to explain. Eyebrows shot up. One man pulled out his cell phone and claimed angrily that he was calling an ambulance whether I liked it or not.

Just then Mama opened her eyes and looked groggily around. I began to knock rapidly on the window and shout, "Mama, Mama! Look at me! Look over here! Over here!" She finally focused on my face and I sharply rapped the glass next to the lock switch. "Mama, Mama! Put your hand on this and pull it, Mama! Right here! Come on, you can do it. Right here! Do it, do it, Mama. Pull it, pull it up!" After a few moments of coaching, Mama's trembling hand slowly rose, and after a few tries, pulled up the lock. She then leaned back, eyes closed in exhaustion. I opened the door and hugged her, then turned to the crowd that has gathered. "I told you..." I started to say, but I was stopped by their expressions of mistrust and amazement.

The man with the cell phone stepped forward, his hands on his hips. "You ARE taking her to the emergency room, aren't you?" He glowered.

"Absolutely not!" I fired back as I got into the driver's seat. "I've had enough of that place to last me a lifetime."

Some of them were shaking their heads as I pulled out, leaving a pert swirl of gravel in my wake.

And so the elephant stumbled and bumbled along.

As psychological stress increased, I sometimes noticed a strange feeling, almost physical, deep within myself. It was an unhinged, floaty sensation that rose in me at strange moments and was quickly gone, like when one turns and catches something out of the corner of one's eye. I was driving home from the grocery store one evening, when Prince's song, *Purple Rain,* came on the radio. I thought about how adept the artist had been at keeping the public's attention by honing down this name from "Prince" to "The Artist Formerly Known as Prince" to "The Artist," and then to a symbol instead of a word. Supposedly, his hieroglyph was a combination of the male and female icons and indicated his bisexuality. I wondered what my symbol would look like. As I pondered this, I suddenly got a mental picture of the strange inner sensation I had been feeling. With my old life disrupted, the hieroglyph that encapsulated who I was, my identity, had changed. A brushstroke, a squiggly line, was missing. The part of me that was known to my parents—me as a baby, me as a child, the nourishment of my constant place in their minds and hearts—was irrevocably gone. The self I had always known had become incomplete. This image filled me with a sense of loss so deep, I had to pull the car to the side of the road and cry. My hieroglyph was unhinged. I was coming apart.

Toppling

About that time, the dreams began. They filtered into my nights so slowly that it took a while for me to realize they formed a repetitive pattern. I had always thought dreams were messages from our subconscious, and perhaps from more exalted places. At certain periods in my life I had filled journals with recorded dreams and possible meanings. The dreams of this period appeared at least two or three times a month, and they were all about caring for baby animals. In each dream, baby animals were given into my care, and in each dream, I failed. I inadvertently smothered, starved, forgot, or injured my charges: the baby owl that I put under my arm for warmth and crushed into a limp sac of splintered bone; the two black kittens that I drowned while trying to bathe them in the tub; the tiny rabbit that I dropped and stepped on while running down a mountain. After each mishap, I suffered boulders of guilt that seemed to sit on my chest for hours even after the relief of waking up. I thought the dreams were transparent. I thought the babies were Mama, and I wasn't giving her the proper care. Yet that interpretation never felt right. Years after Mama's death, a specialist in dreams told me the animals were parts of myself that I was neglecting and I felt that was closer to the truth.

But we trudged on. And it was often redemption that kept us going. Larkin shared a bathroom with Mama, and I also kept some items there, because the bath off the master bedroom was tiny. Larkin's room was beside Mama's. Sometimes I heard my daughter in the night coaching Mama back to bed. "No Grandma, it's not time to get up yet. Everyone is still sleeping. Let me help you back to bed. Come on." Her voice was always kind and calm and I would stay in bed and burrow deep into the covers, congratulating myself on raising a compassionate child.

But one Sunday evening I came home and Larkin was having what our family calls "a breakdown." She came into my room sobbing. "I just can't take this anymore. I can't stand it! I never know what I'll find in the bathroom. My friends were here and there was poop on the sink! What if my boyfriends...if they go in there? And some mornings when I'm late, she won't get out!" She collapsed on the bed and I held onto her, commiserating and praising, remembering what my sister said about building kids' self-esteem: Let them do hard things and then praise them for it.

The moment passed. She continued to share the bathroom and several weeks later she called me to the door. "Look, Mom." She indicated the three objects sitting in a row on the counter—the plastic box with her retainer, my nighttime bite plate in a shallow dish, and Mama's teeth in a glass of water. She grinned. "Three generations!" We hugged each other. Larkin laughed and looked startled when I started to cry.

After that, I realized that tears were always trembling behind my eyes, ready to fall, even in good moments. I also noticed that I had begun to isolate myself from almost everyone who wasn't engaged in my journey with Mama. I shunned social events and, even with old friends, began to feel as though I inhabited another world. At gatherings where people talked and laughed about the doings of normal life, I sat mute, Sylvia in the bell jar.

I remembered when I was photographer for the local paper, how much I enjoyed being such an integral part of the town, how I loved reaching out, talking to people, asking questions. Now my world had shrunk to the size of my house. I didn't want people to come over and disrupt my schedule with Mama or witness my struggle. When Mama was with Beverly, I savored my time alone to do as I pleased, to lick my wounds and gird my strength for the coming weeks.

This journey had begun to lead us into desolate territory, the terrain rocky and uneven. With the quickening steps of the elephant, the three of us were barely hanging on.

At Christmas, Richard and I, Larkin and a friend, were on our way to a ski holiday in Colorado, when I got a call from Bev saying Mama was very ill with viral pneumonia. We changed direction and went to Georgia until the crisis was over. Then the rest of my family went home while I stayed, and Bev and I took turns going to the hospital where Mama was recovering. Sitting beside her bed while she slept, looking out at the dreary Georgia rain, all I wanted was to crawl in beside her, close my eyes and drift with her into a deep forgetfulness.

After she returned to Bev's, too weak to travel, I came home and toppled down into illness. Like Mama, I contracted viral pneumonia and couldn't seem to recover. The phlegm in my lungs lingered for weeks after Mama was supposed to be returned to my care.

The phone calls to and from Georgia flew thick and fast and heavy with bad news. No, I wasn't well yet. Now Bev wasn't feeling well. Mama kicked the sitter that Bev had hired to help take care of her. Perhaps taking his cue from Mama, Bev's dog bit the sitter. No, I wasn't well yet. The sitter called constantly, telling Bev how the bite was swelling, getting infected, draining. Bev paid for the woman's doctor visits, but was afraid she was going to sue. No, I wasn't well yet. Mama had started "sundowning," getting restless and agitated at dusk. She wanted to go home, home, home.

Soon after Mama finally returned to me, Bev toppled. Her blood pressure rose dramatically; her heart palpitated so hard she couldn't get out of bed; she lost her appetite. The doctors diagnosed a "hot spot" on her thyroid. It was biopsied and was benign, but her symptoms continued. We were all weakening. Our grip atop the elephant was being shaken loose.

It was during this time that a friend told me about the new facility that was being built ten minutes from my house. It was part of an existing complex for the elderly and would house an extended care wing, a nursing home, and an Alzheimer's unit. Furthermore, a couple who knew my parents and had attended our church had conceived and built the center. I hustled myself over to the lovely building that spread out in a woodsy, pastoral setting.

I walked into an elegant, clean, light-filled facility. With its charming furniture and beautiful carpeting, it looked more like an upscale hotel than an elder care unit. There were large fish tanks and bird environments, "living rooms" and a beauty parlor, a fenced outdoor area with several gazebos. In the Alzheimer's wing, which was behind locked doors, residents were allowed to move freely about, watch TV or nap in their rooms. There was an activities director and someone who came in to lead exercise classes. The people were friendly and seemed competent.

I returned home from the tour, threw down the brochures and called my sister. "Bev," I joked, "I smell freedom and it smells good."

When did the native family place the elder on the ice floe and push it out into the freezing sea? How exhausted does a soldier have to be before he can no longer carry his wounded comrade? When does the instinct of self-preservation take over and you let go of the hand of someone you love?

We told Mama we were taking her to stay somewhere for a while, somewhere nice, like a vacation. I knew she thought that meant all of us, and I didn't tell her differently. I once read an article about how leaving a parent in a nursing home is an act of violence. That's what it felt like, especially when Mama realized we were leaving and she was to stay behind, alone. She sat down on the side of the bed and gazed down at her narrow feet in her new brown shoes, set one beside the other. In a low voice, she said, "I wish somebody loved me enough to take me home with them." I don't remember much else about that day. Those words were enough.

Paul

Mama settled into the routine of the facility as well as could be expected. She often referred to it as her "school." Her daily life, the present moment, was more real to her than any memories of the past. Of course, there were times of upset and anxiety. When I visited, I came away with mixed emotions: guilt, worry, relief. I felt Mama was safe, but I felt strangely at a loss without her. It would take more than sleeping through the night to restore the broken hieroglyph of myself, and I wished Mama could help guide me through this transition. In some ways, she seemed to be doing better than I was.

When we were growing up, if there was news of a suicide, Mama would tell us, "Never give up on life. You never know what's right around the corner." Whenever she began to recover from one of life's hard passages, like her mastectomy, Mama would say, "I feel my strength coming back to me. It's time for me to rise up." It was as if she had the utmost confidence in life, in her strength, her ability to rise. It was just a matter of the right time. At ninety-one years old, her brain blunted with disease, living in a nursing home, Mama didn't give up. She recovered her strength and rose up enough to fall in love. His name was Paul.

I pressed the code numbers on the pad to enter the Alzheimer's wing and walked into the sunny hall. In the common room, four residents sat in front of a strident TV with their eyes closed and heads bent forward to their chests, reminding me of a short row of wilted sunflowers. Mama's room stood empty and tidy, the large stuffed bunny a friend had brought sitting upright in her armchair. I checked the sunny area at the end of the hall, but there was only a new resident running her fingers over the window sashes and murmuring softly as though reading a story in Braille. The bathing area was also empty. A small whirlwind of panic started in my chest. I went to the nurse's station and they told me to check some of the other rooms.

Through the door of the third room I saw a man I knew only as Paul, sitting sideways on his bed, lounging against the headboard. He was short and neatly dressed with a large head of white wavy hair and a barrel chest. I had noticed Paul because of his demeanor. Instead of appearing dazed and feeble like so many of the residents, Paul still exuded vital body energy and had a slightly imperious air about him. He was staring straight ahead at nothing.

I pushed open the door and Mama was sitting beside the bed in a chair. Dressed in one of her best outfits, her feet were propped up on the foot of Paul's bed like two primly dressed dolls. She was staring at Paul.

"Mama! There you are. I couldn't find you."

She turned slightly to look at me without moving her legs. "Oh..." She hesitated, not sure who I was.

"Are you visiting Paul?" I pulled up a straight back chair and sat beside her.

"Oh, yes." She smiled happily, the smile of a much younger woman. Paul's stare traveled over me without the slightest interest, then returned to his air gaze.

"Look Mama. I've brought your favorite candy." I brought out a small box of chocolates.

"Oh, good!" In one smooth motion, Mama took the box, whipped off the top and passed it to Paul. "Won't you have some?" she asked breathlessly, her voice as sweet as the candy.

Paul considered the offering, then slowly took a dark chocolate and chewed it. A small smile creased his lips. Mama looked at me and raised her eyebrows as if to say how lucky we were that he liked candy. She and I each ate a piece and then the box was again passed to Paul. He declined and Mama placed the box beside him on the coverlet with a small pat.

I put my arm around her. "Mama, let's go back to your room. I've brought Jenga and some puzzles and then I'll take you out to lunch."

Mama shifted away and looked fondly at Paul. "Oh, no. I think I'll just stay here with…with…" For a moment she frowned with confusion, then smiled, "…with HIM."

I knew I should stay and make conversation, but I found myself back in the hall, my head tight and pounding. A nurse, passing with a tray of pills, inquired. "Did you find her?"

I forced myself to smile. "Oh, yes. In Paul's room. I think she's found a friend."

She laughed. "Yes. They've become quite an item. They were trying to escape the other day, standing hand in hand in front of the door. Anytime it opened, they tried to get out."

I went in Mama's room and sat on her bed, not understanding why I felt so sad, so angry. *You should be ecstatic. You should be relieved. What's wrong with you?* Then that floaty feeling crept back into my midsection, and tears slid down my cheeks. The mangled hieroglyphic spun above me in the air. *First, not known and now, not even needed.* I jumped up. I did not want to think these thoughts. All I wanted to do was get away.

In Mama's bathroom I splashed cold water on my eyes. I didn't recognize the face reflected in the mirror. I looked pale and fat and aged beyond my years. I looked lost.

I stumbled out into the hall, hoping I could get back to the car without having to talk to anyone. As I neared the door, the new resident, who had been at the end of the hall earlier, came out of the common room and accosted me. She gripped my arm with both hands, her thin fingers like iron, her white hair awry. Her eyes were frantic and rheumy, her lower lip trembled and she smelled like her diaper.

"Oh please tell me, can you tell me, can you tell me who I AM...oh please, can you tell me, can you tell me..." Her fetid breath was suffocating.

I grabbed her hands to push her away. *I've got to get out of here. I can't stand these people another minute. I want out!* But she wouldn't let go. Her fingernails dug into my arm, and her knees knocked into mine.

Giving up, I stopped struggling and looked into her eyes. And gazing back at me, I saw the same expression I had just seen in the mirror, the same emotion I had seen in Mama's eyes when she had asked her sequence of questions. At that moment in time, we were not sure who we were, or why we were. We were lost. After a moment of staring, I pulled the woman to me and held her tightly, my tears flowing. We stood there, rocking back and forth. The faces I had seen at funerals, on the news after a disaster, even gazing out of a bus window, streamed through my brain. I thought of the age-old philosophical question, "Who am I?" Thoughts from my spiritual search flooded in: Buddha's realization that in every life there is suffering, the Christian idea that suffering brings you to the feet of Jesus, the Goddess belief that the Goddess is immanent in all things, even suffering.

The tightness inside my head began to melt and then this woman said the most wonderful thing. She leaned back her head and looked at me. She was drooling. She was beaming. "You love me, then." It was more a statement than a question.

I smiled back at her. "Yes," I said quietly, "I love you." And she put her head back on my chest and we rocked some more. And as I rocked her, I was rocking myself, rocking Mama, rocking all who were lost.

In a moment the two nurses came out of their station, peeled the woman off my chest and coaxed her down the hall to her room. I wiped my eyes and went back to Paul's room. Paul was asleep, pitched sideways on the bed, snoring. Mama sat where I left her, but she was holding the box of chocolates.

"Mama," I exclaimed. "It's a beautiful day! Let's go out somewhere nice for lunch."

She studied me quickly. "All right," she answered gaily as she proffered the candy. "Won't you have some?"

That night in bed, I rehashed the day in my mind. I felt good, settled—as though I had been through a passage and was striving to understand it. As I lay there, the hieroglyphic came into my mind's eye. It dangled there, turning slowly before me, and I saw that the missing brushstroke, the squiggly line, had been restored, but looked different. The shape was deeper, wider, the stroke more distinct, the color richer. And I understood that part of my personal signature, my small journey, had been replaced with one of a more universal nature that connected me with all people. One that bore the experience of suffering, infused with the human stain of compassion. I had moved from the personal into a larger domain, where I was more than I had been before.

Fly Away Home

It had been five months since Mama entered the facility. Although I was worried about Beverly, who was still shaky, I was able to rest in this new context, rest in the fact that Mama had something of a life and that *my* life had enlarged. I was starting to reform my eating and exercise habits and trying to integrate myself into a work routine. Then the phone call came saying that Mama had fallen and broken her hip. The facility had called the ambulance and I was to go directly to the hospital. I asked the nurse how it had happened and she said someone had pushed Mama down, but she wouldn't tell me who. That was "protected" information. I grabbed my sweater and ran.

Mama's face against the pillow was as pale as bone. She was drugged and didn't know I was there. The doctor was talking to me about making a choice concerning her hip, but he seemed tiny and far away. I felt as though I watched him through the wrong end of a telescope. We could let the hip heal as it was and she would be bedridden, or she could have an operation and a chance to walk again. He said she was in good shape for her age, and they thought she could stand an operation. I unearthed my cell phone and called my sister. After much consultation, Bev and I decided Mama would have taken the possibility of being back on her feet.

The following month and a half remains a blur in my mind, with some things stuck in my memory. I recall sitting with Richard outside the ICU after the operation. We thought Mama was dying and prayed for her to be taken swiftly, for her suffering to be curbed. But sometime in the night, Mama rallied and asked for water. Then the suffering really began.

Mama's mind couldn't process the fact that she had had an operation and that she needed to rest. Once I walked into the hospital room and she was halfway out of bed, clawing off the bandage on her hip, while blood and fluids soaked the bed. She didn't remember why "that rag" was stuck to her body, making it ache. We went into constant care mode. The sitters returned. Most of them were wonderful people, invaluable helpmates.

We moved her back to the nursing home and despite frequent turnings she developed a bedsore on her behind that was so deep I could see down to her tailbone. The nurses explained that if she were ever to walk again, Mama would soon have to be back on her feet. Therefore, she couldn't be totally doped up with pain medication. Without the drugs she suffered, often not understanding where she was or why she hurt. But true to her nature, Mama didn't give up. When I explained to her that in order to walk again, she had to get up and practice, she did. The aides and I sat her up on the edge of the bed for a short period each day. Then, using a walker, we moved her to sit in a chair. The next time, she took a few steps. One day she walked almost to the bathroom, about twelve steps. For the first time she smiled at my praise. But her wound wasn't healing as well as it should and Mama was suffering. Her moans and cries when she was bathed or when the aides had to lift her to weigh her, were so piteous that I couldn't stay in the room. Bev and I agonized about our decision. The future stretched out before us, long and dim. When and if she recovered her walking ability, what would her life be like? As Bev said, sometimes we didn't know what to hope for.

Twice Mama had to travel by ambulance back to doctors' offices for checkups. Both trips left me feeling helpless with anger. I was angry at a system that did not ask the doctor to drive the three miles from his office to the nursing home. I thought Mama was kept too long in waiting rooms. It seemed she was handled too roughly for someone in her condition and left to lie exposed in chilly air for long periods. I was angry with myself because I felt paralyzed in the face of the medical establishment. Was I too weak to rant and rave? Had I given up? Once when I was younger and couldn't seem to stand up for myself, Mama said I had "a heart of mush, covered in gold leaf." I learned that an older person going through medical procedures needs an advocate constantly by her side. Not being more of an aggressive advocate for Mama is one my few regrets, one that will always haunt me.

I believe Mama decided, after one of these trips, that enough was enough. She began to refuse food and spit out her pills. She sank more and more into herself. Mama was moving away from life. Without consulting each other, Bev and I had the same feeling one night—that it was time to let go and allow Mama to leave this world. We contacted Hospice. I sat with the helpful representative and felt as if I heard everything she said through a sieve; nothing seemed to fall solidly together. But I was grateful, especially for the morphine Hospice provided. Sometimes I didn't know if I was asking the nurses to give the drug to Mama because of her suffering, or because of how I suffered watching her struggle. I called in my friends to take turns sitting with Mama, and they came. I wanted someone I knew to be with her if she slipped away when I wasn't there.

Bev and her children came and we clung together. Bev looked wan. She had lost weight and her hands shook.

For several days we crowded around Mama, stroking her hands, telling her who we were, singing hymns and old songs she loved, "In the Garden," "Beulah Land," "Moon River." She seemed to recognize that we were people who loved her, but mostly she lay with her eyes closed.

When it came time to tell Mama it was OK to let go, the words stuck in my throat. I knelt by her bed and remembered how she had urged me into my life's adventures, even when she was concerned about my safety. "Go, chile, go!" she would say with a bright, sometimes forced, smile. I leaned close and clutched her hand. "It's OK," I whispered, "you can go. You can fly away. I'll be fine. Go, Mama, go!" She didn't respond, but I thought I felt a slight pressure from her fingers.

When her eyes were open, Mama seemed to look past us, as if looking into a reality we couldn't see. Once, she leaned up and began reaching out in front of herself again and again with her hands. As I had just been thinking of Daddy, I asked, "Are you reaching for Hobart?" She barely nodded and sank back on the pillows.

When I related that moment to Bev, she told me that as they left Athens, a red-tailed hawk, the bird that Daddy loved, had swooped low in front of their car. Bev reminded me that soon after Daddy died, she had been driving to Blacksburg on the highway that climbs steeply into the mountains. A red-tailed hawk sat on a tree branch over the road. It seemed to be tracking the car, watching Bev fixedly. My sister, who does not usually have mystical experiences, said an intense feeling swept through her that the hawk was Daddy, watching over her. She sobbed all the way up the mountain. When she told Sarah about the hawk, Sarah shared her own experience of the hawk looking in the basement window in Georgia, and the poem that she had written.

Mama was weakening. October twenty-ninth, when Sarah and I came in to take the morning shift, we felt Mama's transition was near. Her breathing was shallow. Her skin had settled onto her face so that you could clearly see the shape of the skull underneath. I had heard people call this "the death mask" and relate it as a sign of impending demise. After a very emotional morning, Richard, Sarah and I went to my house to eat lunch and try to nap while Bev took over the vigil. As we looked out my back window, there were some small birds on a tree and I remarked how birds are harbingers of joy, and how Mama and Daddy used to watch the birds at their feeder.

Sarah walked into the living room and out of the corner of her eye, saw a big bird dive down in front of the window. She thought it was just a crow or woodpecker, some other bird that might frequent a suburban yard. Richard and I were getting some blankets out for naps when suddenly there was a loud squawking outside. It was a ruckus we couldn't ignore. Sarah went to the front door and looked out of the small panes. At first she saw only a jay in the bush right outside. It was screeching madly. Then Sarah saw a very large bird on the ground just beside the stoop, about three feet from the door. It was holding its wings out protectively.

She called us to come look and Richard said, "That's a red-tailed hawk!" We couldn't believe it. A hawk had come right down to the front door, and a blue jay had announced its presence. The two birds stayed there while we watched through the window, the jay still screeching, and the hawk holding out its wings. We finally opened the door and both birds flew up. The blue jay disappeared, but the hawk flew back to us. As we stood in the yard, the hawk circled above us. It circled round and round as we held on to each other and cried. Then it began a slow ascent, spiraling up until it was a dot, and then flying into the blinding white disc of the sun.

We will always think of the hawk as Daddy, coming for Mama, coming to ease our hearts, for Mama took flight that evening, her spirit slipping easily away.

For several weeks afterward, mostly as I stood in my kitchen, I felt Mama move in beside me. The feeling was so real, so palpable, that I would turn and say, "Mama! Hello!" And she stayed with me a while and I would bask in the feeling of her, all my dark musings turning to light.

Then one night I had a dream. I dreamt I was coming up the walkway to my home when I looked down and saw a large, dead bird in front of me. I picked it up and carried it into the house. I was holding the cold carcass in my hands when it became warmer and warmer and finally began to stir. The bird had come alive again and I began caressing its soft body over and over, stroking the feathers, feeling the tiny pulse of the beating heart. Oh, how I loved, how I wanted to keep, that bird. But the bird began to struggle and I knew it didn't belong to me, that I had to let it go. I opened the door and the bird rose out of my hands and flew away into a nearby woods. I never felt Mama beside me again.

I like to imagine it sometimes. I see Daddy as the handsome red-tail, robust and courageous enough to break through the barrier between the worlds. He is soaring up toward the sun, and behind the hawk, flapping its wide ears, flies a huge elephant. This is no cartoon pachyderm. The hide hangs tattered and pockmarked. Its square feet are worn and bruised. The backbone sticks up in a ragged line, but atop its back, a diminutive figure sits straight, her eyes wide, her mind as clear as crystal. Mama is holding on, as usual, for the ride.

Helpful Resources

National Alzheimer's Association
www.alz.org
An extremely helpful, informative and pleasing website with connections to local organizations, a library, and email news.

Alzheimer's Foundation
www.alzfdn.org
Provides lists of dementia care facilities that have been evaluated and have achieved their "Excellence In Care" Status. Their free quarterly magazine, *ADvantage*, provides useful and interesting information.

A Place for Mom
www.aplaceformom.com
Provides a referral service by location to dementia care facilities; includes forums and blogs.

Alzheimer's Disease International
www.alz.co.uk
Provides tips for care givers and connections to Alzheimer's Associations in many countries.

Caregiver Products
www.CareGiverProducts.com
Wonderful assortment of products for sale to help care for a dementia patient.

Alzheimer's Disease Education & Referral Center
www.alzheimers.org
A great resource for finding the latest research information, helpful drugs, etc.

Diane Porter Goff is a writer and photographer who lives in the Virginia mountains with her husband, Richard. She holds a Master's degree from Hollins University. Her work has appeared in *The Sun, Southern Distinctions, Magical Blend,* and in the anthology, *Beyond Forgetting: Poetry and Prose about Alzheimer's Disease,* among other venues. She has taught workshops for The Reynolds Homestead, The Light Factory and, in Greece, the Ariadne Institute. She traveled and performed as a member of WEB 6, a group of artists, writers and singers. Her photography has been exhibited in the Mies van der Rohe House in Chicago, the Ledel Gallery in New York, the Touchstone Gallery in Washington D.C. and the Virginia Museum in Richmond. As photographer and videographer for Company of Women, she worked with a group of international actresses, writer Carole Gilligan, voice teacher Kristin Linklater and director Maureen Shea. She served as guest artist at the Penland School in North Carolina.

To contact Diane, visit her Web site at:

www.RidingTheElephantMemoir.com